P9-AOH-418

The Declaration of Independence

A Model for Individual Rights

Titles in the
Words That Changed History series include:

The Declaration of Independence
The Emancipation Proclamation
The Nuremberg Laws
The Origin of Species
The U.S. Constitution

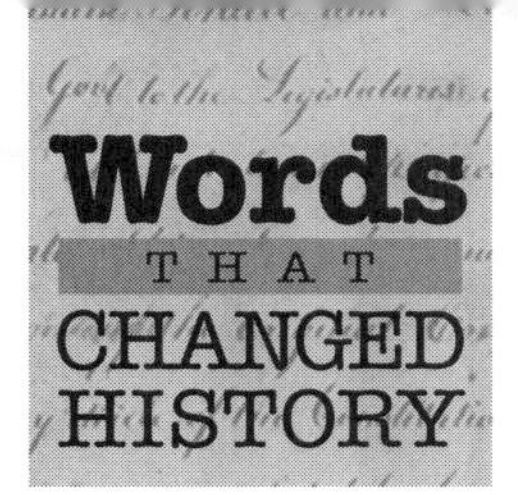

The Declaration of Independence

A Model for Individual Rights

by Don Nardo

Lucent Books
P.O. Box 289011, San Diego, CA 92198-9011

Library of Congress Cataloging-in-Publication Data

Nardo, Don, 1947–
The Declaration of Independence : a model for individual rights / by Don Nardo.
p. cm. — (Words that changed history series)
Includes bibliographical references (p.) and index.
Summary: Discusses the drafting, composition, symbolism, ideas, and influence of the Declaration of Independence.
ISBN 1-56006-368-8 (lib. : alk. paper)
1. United States. Declaration of Independence—Juvenile literature. 2. United States—Politics and government—1775–1783—Juvenile literature. [1. United States. Declaration of Independence. 2. United States—Politics and government—1775–1783.] I. Title. II. Series.
E221.N25 1999
973.3'13—dc21 98-7338
CIP
AC

P.O. Box 289011, San Diego, California 92198-9011

Printed in the U.S.A.

Contents

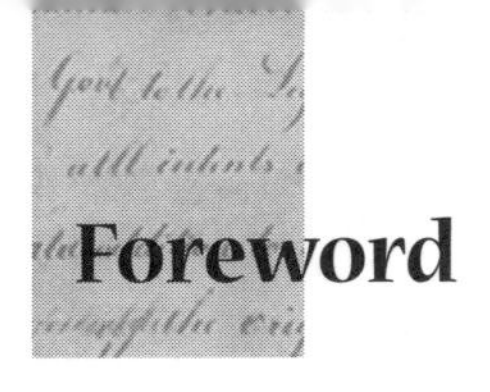

Foreword

"We hold these truths to be self-evident, that all men are created equal, that they are endowed by their Creator with certain unalienable Rights, that among these are Life, Liberty and the pursuit of Happiness." So states one of America's most cherished documents, the Declaration of Independence. These words ripple through time. They represent the thoughts of the Declaration's author, Thomas Jefferson, but at the same time they reflect the attitudes of a nation in which individual rights were trampled by a foreign government. To many of Jefferson's contemporaries, these words characterized a revolutionary philosophy of liberty. Many Americans today still believe the ideas expressed in the Declaration were uniquely American. And while it is true that this document was a product of American ideals and values, its ideas did not spring from an intellectual vacuum. The Enlightenment which had pervaded France and England for years had proffered ideas of individual rights, and Enlightenment scholars drew their notions from historical antecedents tracing back to ancient Greece.

In essence, the Declaration was part of an ongoing historical dialogue concerning the conflict between individual rights and government powers. There is no doubt, however, that it made a palpable impact on its times. For colonists, the Declaration listed their grievances and set out the ideas for which they would stand and fight. These words changed history for Americans. But the Declaration also changed history for other nations; in France, revolutionaries would emulate concepts of self-rule to bring down their own monarchy and draft their own philosophies in a document known as the Declaration of the Rights of Man and of the Citizen. And the historical dialogue continues today in many third world nations.

Lucent Books's Words That Changed History series looks at oral and written documents in light of their historical context and their lasting impact. Some documents, such as the Declaration, spurred people to immediately change society; other documents fostered lasting intellectual debate. For example, Charles Darwin's treatise *On the Origin of Species* did not simply extend the discussion of human origins, it offered a theory of evolution which eventually would cause a schism between some religious and scientific thinkers. The debate still rages as people on both sides reaffirm their intellectual positions, even as new scientific evidence continues to impact the issue.

Students researching famous documents, the time periods in which they were prominent, or the issues they raise will find the books in this series both compelling and useful. Readers will see the chain of events that give rise to historical events. They will understand through the examination of specific documents that ideas or philosophies always have their antecedents, and they will learn how these documents carried on the legacy of influence by affecting people in other places or other times. The format for the series emphasizes these points by devoting chapters to the political or intellectual climate of the times, the values and prejudices of the drafters or speakers, the contents of the document and its impact on its contemporaries, and the manner in which perceptions of the document have changed through time.

In addition to their format, the books in Lucent's Words That Changed History series contain features that enhance understanding. Many primary and secondary source quotes give readers insight into the thoughts of the document's contemporaries as well as those who interpret the document's significance in hindsight. Sidebars interspersed throughout the text offer greater examination of relevant personages or significant events to provide readers with a broader historical context. Footnotes allow readers to verify the credibility of source material. Two bibliographies give students the opportunity to expand their research. And an appendix that includes excerpts as well as full text of original documents give students access to the larger historical picture into which these documents fit.

History is often shaped by words. Oral and written documents concretize the thoughts of a select few, but they often transform the beliefs of an entire era or nation. As Confucius asserted, "Without knowing the force of words, it is impossible to know men." And understanding the power of words reveals a new way of understanding history.

Introduction

The Documentary Symbol of American Union

On August 10, 1776, the town councilmen of Savannah, Georgia, gathered in their chamber and listened to the president of the council read the stirring words of the Declaration of Independence, printed copies of which had recently spread throughout the former British American colonies. The men then hurried to the local town meetinghouse and read the document to a crowd of eager citizens. Not long afterward, they read it still again at the town square, as described in this surviving eyewitness account:

> They were met by the Georgia Battalion [local militia] who, after reading of the Declaration, discharged their field pieces and fired in platoons. Upon this they proceeded to the Battery [artillery area] . . . where the Declaration was read for the last time, and the cannon of the Battery discharged. . . . Everyone dined . . . and cheerfully drank to the United Free and Independent States of America. . . . My friends and fellow citizens . . . let us remember that America is free and independent; that she is, and will be, with the blessing of the Almighty, great among the nations of the earth. . . . May God give us blessing, and let all the people say Amen! [1]

It should be noted that festivities like these, which took place in towns in all of the states of the new American union, celebrated America's newfound independence, not the Declaration of Independence itself. At the time, the document was seen as little more than the means of announcing the momentous news of separation from the mother country. Yet over the course of time the Declaration became world famous, enormously influential, and even revered. "No other American document," remarks the distinguished American historian Dumas Malone, "has been read so often or listened to by so many weary and perspiring audiences. Yet, despite interminable repetition, those well-worn phrases have never lost their potency and charm." [2]

In retrospect, the reasons for the document's enduring popularity are not hard to fathom. First, it was, after all, more than just a statement of independence. Over the course of history, many revolutionaries have expressed their grievances against their oppressors and declared themselves free and independent; but few have, in the process, as the American founders did, stated profound moral truths that could readily be applied to people in all ages. As one of America's greatest presidents, Abraham Lincoln, later wrote:

> All honor to Jefferson—to the man, who in the concrete pressure of a struggle for national independence by a single people, had the coolness . . . and sagacity [perceptive judgment] to introduce into a merely revolutionary document an abstract truth, applicable to all men and all times.[3]

This famous painting by illustrator Howard Pyle shows a soldier reading the recently completed Declaration of Independence to George Washington's army on July 9, 1776.

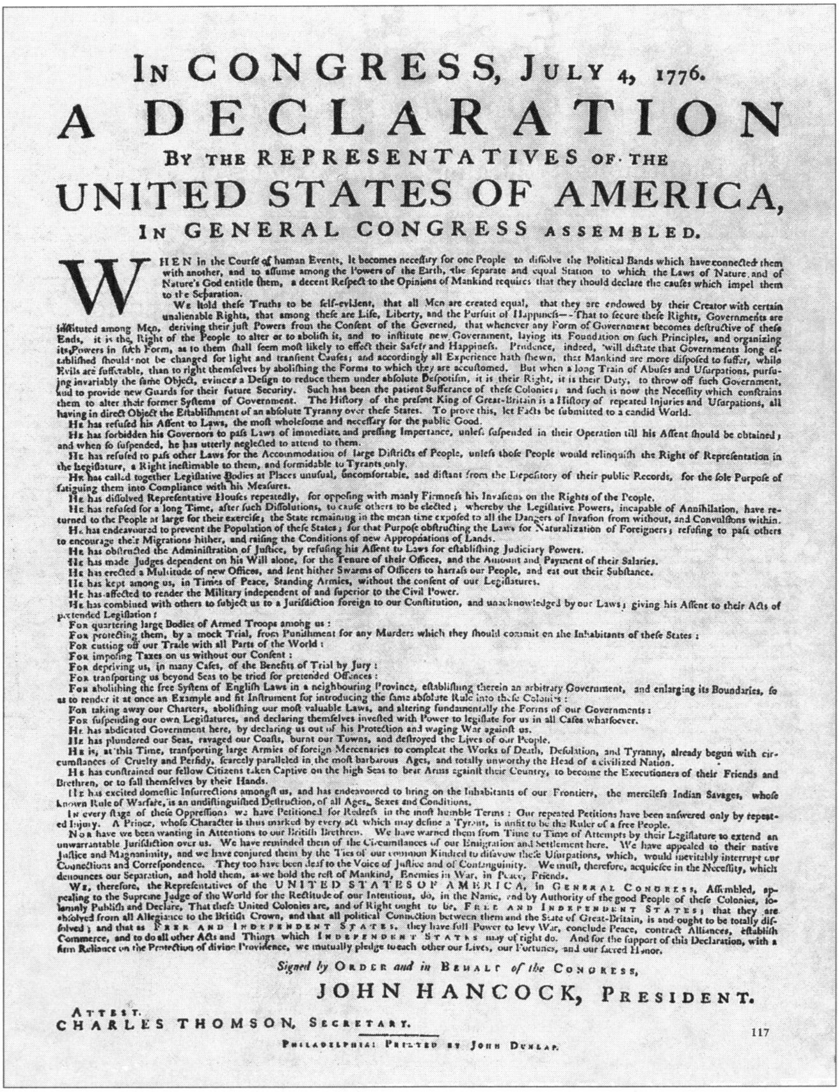

IN CONGRESS, JULY 4, 1776.

A DECLARATION

BY THE REPRESENTATIVES OF THE

UNITED STATES OF AMERICA,

IN GENERAL CONGRESS ASSEMBLED.

WHEN in the Course of human Events, it becomes necessary for one People to dissolve the Political Bands which have connected them with another, and to assume among the Powers of the Earth, the separate and equal Station to which the Laws of Nature and of Nature's God entitle them, a decent Respect to the Opinions of Mankind requires that they should declare the causes which impel them to the Separation.

WE hold these Truths to be self-evident, that all Men are created equal, that they are endowed by their Creator with certain unalienable Rights, that among these are Life, Liberty, and the Pursuit of Happiness—That to secure these Rights, Governments are instituted among Men, deriving their just Powers from the Consent of the Governed, that whenever any Form of Government becomes destructive of these Ends, it is the Right of the People to alter or to abolish it, and to institute new Government, laying its Foundation on such Principles, and organizing its Powers in such Form, as to them shall seem most likely to effect their Safety and Happiness. Prudence, indeed, will dictate that Governments long established should not be changed for light and transient Causes; and accordingly all Experience hath shewn, that Mankind are more disposed to suffer, while Evils are sufferable, than to right themselves by abolishing the Forms to which they are accustomed. But when a long Train of Abuses and Usurpations, pursuing invariably the same Object, evinces a Design to reduce them under absolute Despotism, it is their Right, it is their Duty, to throw off such Government, and to provide new Guards for their future Security. Such has been the patient Sufferance of these Colonies; and such is now the Necessity which constrains them to alter their former Systems of Government. The History of the present King of Great-Britain is a History of repeated Injuries and Usurpations, all having in direct Object the Establishment of an absolute Tyranny over these States. To prove this, let Facts be submitted to a candid World.

HE has refused his Assent to Laws, the most wholesome and necessary for the public Good.

HE has forbidden his Governors to pass Laws of immediate and pressing Importance, unless suspended in their Operation till his Assent should be obtained; and when so suspended, he has utterly neglected to attend to them.

HE has refused to pass other Laws for the Accommodation of large Districts of People, unless those People would relinquish the Right of Representation in the Legislature, a Right inestimable to them, and formidable to Tyrants only.

HE has called together Legislative Bodies at Places unusual, uncomfortable, and distant from the Depository of their public Records, for the sole Purpose of fatiguing them into Compliance with his Measures.

HE has dissolved Representative Houses repeatedly, for opposing with manly Firmness his Invasions on the Rights of the People.

HE has refused for a long Time, after such Dissolutions, to cause others to be elected; whereby the Legislative Powers, incapable of Annihilation, have returned to the People at large for their exercise; the State remaining in the mean time exposed to all the Dangers of Invasion from without, and Convulsions within.

HE has endeavoured to prevent the Population of these States; for that Purpose obstructing the Laws for Naturalization of Foreigners; refusing to pass others to encourage their Migrations hither, and raising the Conditions of new Appropriations of Lands.

HE has obstructed the Administration of Justice, by refusing his Assent to Laws for establishing Judiciary Powers.

HE has made Judges dependent on his Will alone, for the Tenure of their Offices, and the Amount and Payment of their Salaries.

HE has erected a Multitude of new Offices, and sent hither Swarms of Officers to harrass our People, and eat out their Substance.

HE has kept among us, in Times of Peace, Standing Armies, without the consent of our Legislatures.

HE has affected to render the Military independent of and superior to the Civil Power.

HE has combined with others to subject us to a Jurisdiction foreign to our Constitution, and unacknowledged by our Laws; giving his Assent to their Acts of pretended Legislation:

FOR quartering large Bodies of Armed Troops among us:

FOR protecting them, by a mock Trial, from Punishment for any Murders which they should commit on the Inhabitants of these States:

FOR cutting off our Trade with all Parts of the World:

FOR imposing Taxes on us without our Consent:

FOR depriving us, in many Cases, of the Benefits of Trial by Jury:

FOR transporting us beyond Seas to be tried for pretended Offences:

FOR abolishing the free System of English Laws in a neighbouring Province, establishing therein an arbitrary Government, and enlarging its Boundaries, so as to render it at once an Example and fit Instrument for introducing the same absolute Rule into these Colonies:

FOR taking away our Charters, abolishing our most valuable Laws, and altering fundamentally the Forms of our Governments:

FOR suspending our own Legislatures, and declaring themselves invested with Power to legislate for us in all Cases whatsoever.

HE has abdicated Government here, by declaring us out of his Protection and waging War against us.

HE has plundered our Seas, ravaged our Coasts, burnt our Towns, and destroyed the Lives of our People.

HE is, at this Time, transporting large Armies of foreign Mercenaries to compleat the Works of Death, Desolation, and Tyranny, already begun with circumstances of Cruelty and Perfidy, scarcely paralleled in the most barbarous Ages, and totally unworthy the Head of a civilized Nation.

HE has constrained our fellow Citizens taken Captive on the high Seas to bear Arms against their Country, to become the Executioners of their Friends and Brethren, or to fall themselves by their Hands.

HE has excited domestic Insurrections amongst us, and has endeavoured to bring on the Inhabitants of our Frontiers, the merciless Indian Savages, whose known Rule of Warfare, is an undistinguished Destruction, of all Ages, Sexes and Conditions.

IN every stage of these Oppressions we have Petitioned for Redress in the most humble Terms: Our repeated Petitions have been answered only by repeated Injury. A Prince, whose Character is thus marked by every act which may define a Tyrant, is unfit to be the Ruler of a free People.

NOR have we been wanting in Attentions to our British Brethren. We have warned them from Time to Time of Attempts by their Legislature to extend an unwarrantable Jurisdiction over us. We have reminded them of the Circumstances of our Emigration and Settlement here. We have appealed to their native Justice and Magnanimity, and we have conjured them by the Ties of our common Kindred to disavow these Usurpations, which, would inevitably interrupt our Connections and Correspondence. They too have been deaf to the Voice of Justice and of Consanguinity. We must, therefore, acquiesce in the Necessity, which denounces our Separation, and hold them, as we hold the rest of Mankind, Enemies in War, in Peace, Friends.

WE, therefore, the Representatives of the UNITED STATES OF AMERICA, in GENERAL CONGRESS, Assembled, appealing to the Supreme Judge of the World for the Rectitude of our Intentions, do, in the Name, and by Authority of the good People of these Colonies, solemnly Publish and Declare, That these United Colonies are, and of Right ought to be, FREE AND INDEPENDENT STATES; that they are absolved from all Allegiance to the British Crown, and that all political Connection between them and the State of Great-Britain, is and ought to be totally dissolved; and that as FREE AND INDEPENDENT STATES, they have full Power to levy War, conclude Peace, contract Alliances, establish Commerce, and to do all other Acts and Things which INDEPENDENT STATES may of right do. And for the support of this Declaration, with a firm Reliance on the Protection of divine Providence, we mutually pledge to each other our Lives, our Fortunes, and our sacred Honor.

Signed by ORDER *and in* BEHALF *of the* CONGRESS,

JOHN HANCOCK, PRESIDENT.

ATTEST.
CHARLES THOMSON, SECRETARY.

117

PHILADELPHIA: PRINTED BY JOHN DUNLAP.

Contrary to popular belief, most of the founding fathers signed the Declaration in August, not July, 1776. This early printed copy, issued by John Dunlop, appeared in 1777.

Indeed, the Declaration's opening words, "When, in the course of human events," boldly placed the struggle of the American patriots against a background not only of British and American events, but also of global history. And it was not British or American laws that the document invoked, but those of "Nature and Nature's God." The noted scholar of American history, Henry Steele Commager, points out, "No other political document of the eighteenth century proclaimed so broad a purpose; no political document of our own day associates the United States so boldly with universal history and the cosmic system."[4]

Besides being the most quoted statement of human rights in recorded history, the Declaration also laid down, in a few simple and elegant statements of principle, the fundamental precepts for creating a new and democratic form of government. In phrases such as "all men are created equal," "inalienable rights," and "governments . . . deriving their just powers from the consent of the governed," states acclaimed Jefferson biographer Joseph J. Ellis, the document constituted "the seminal statement of the American Creed, the closest approximation to political poetry ever produced in American culture."[5] In a mere few hundred words, the Declaration espoused both a concise political philosophy justifying the authority of the state and defining fundamental rights under the law, and an ethical philosophy defining the happiness of individual citizens as the ultimate end of government.

For these reasons, the Declaration has become, in a sense, the documentary symbol of the American union. In their daring statement of independence, most of the founders almost certainly did not imagine that they were setting in motion a process that would eventually create the world's freest democracy and strongest nation. Yet John Adams, one of the most farsighted of their number, captured a fleeting vision of the future in a letter he wrote to his wife, Abigail, on July 3, 1776, the day before the Declaration's ratification:

> You will think me transported with enthusiasm, but I am not. I am well aware of the toil, and blood, and treasure, that it will cost us to maintain this declaration, and support and defend these States. Yet, through all the gloom, I can see the rays of ravishing light and glory. I can see that the end is more than worth all the means, and that posterity will triumph in that day's transaction, even although we should rue [regret] it, which I trust in God we shall not.[6]

Chapter 1 The Origins and Growth of the Spirit of '76

Thomas Jefferson, the principal author of the Declaration of Independence, was born in Virginia in 1743. By then that British colony was already 136 years old.[7] As a young man, Jefferson, like his relatives and friends, had few complaints with the mother country, in spite of several restrictive policies that nation had imposed on its colonies over the years. Between the mid-1600s and mid-1700s, for example, Britain had imposed a series of trade laws, collectively called the Navigation Acts, generally designed to allow it to control and reap the benefits of colonial trade. These laws mandated that cargo ships had to be built and manned by British or colonial sailors and all goods had to be shipped to England first, regardless of their ultimate destination. This forced the colonists to pay higher prices. But in general, the American response to such restrictions was to accept grudgingly the moderate and less bothersome ones and to evade the more extreme and annoying ones. For instance, when the British enacted the Molasses Act in 1733, which threatened the lucrative trade between New England and the West Indies, American shippers began smuggling in foreign molasses. Thus the law, which was not very well enforced, became null and void in practice.

Despite the Navigation Acts, then, the colonies flourished and grew, both in wealth and population. By 1700, their combined population had reached 250,000. That total would continue to climb, attaining an astounding growth rate of 25 percent per decade by the time of Jefferson's childhood and reaching some 2,250,000 persons by 1775, at the onset of the Revolutionary War. The upshot was that, until the early 1760s, when Jefferson was in his late teens and early twenties, all Americans, even those who disliked and/or evaded British regulations, considered themselves British subjects and did not in the least entertain the idea of separating from the mother country.

However, many colonists underwent a drastic change of attitude during what turned out to be the formative stage of the Revolution, beginning in earnest with the Stamp Act in 1765 and ending with the outbreak of hostilities in 1775. In this crucial period, the British imposed several acts that the colonists viewed as much more restrictive and outrageous than any of the Navigation Acts. And as noted historian Richard Hofstadter suggests, "the friction engendered" by these policies "went far to encourage the spirit of restless independence that erupted in 1776."[8]

Yet it is important to realize that the so-called "spirit of '76" did not infect everyone and that most Americans did not seriously consider the notion of independence until shortly before they achieved it. Many colonists remained loyal to the mother country (and so became known as loyalists), some of them preferring to leave America rather than relinquish their identities as Englishmen. And right up until the

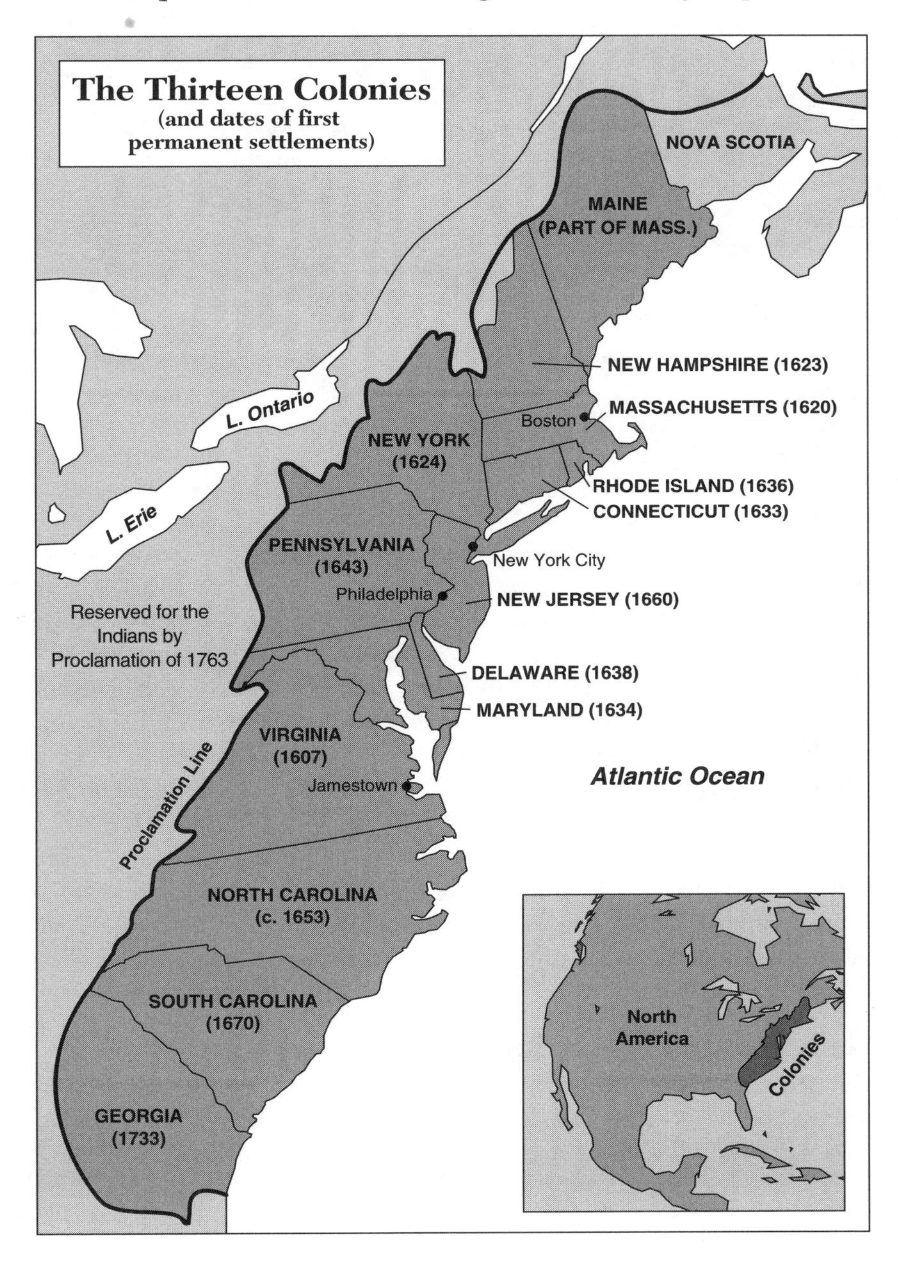

Patrick Henry delivers his stirring and now famous "Give me liberty or give me death" speech to the Virginia state assembly on March 23, 1775.

proverbial last minute—that is, until the approval of the Declaration of Independence on July 4, 1776—most American patriots remained uncertain and divided. Even after the war's opening volleys of musket fire, some, including Thomas Jefferson and George Washington, hoped for some kind of reconciliation with Britain. At this time these men did not in their hearts want independence from the mother country. Rather, they only desired to be accorded their full rights as Englishmen, rights they felt that Parliament had lately unjustly abridged.

By contrast, in the face of what they saw as outrageous British abuses, radicals such as Samuel Adams, Patrick Henry, and Thomas Paine argued for a split from Britain. Paine, for example, pointed out that Britain taxed its American colonies to finance its wars. Since Britain's wars were not America's wars, Britain and America ought to part company. This was the supercharged ideological and emotional atmosphere that existed in the months and weeks preceding the Declaration of Independence.

The Problem of Paying for the Troops

The dramatic, immediate series of events that created that atmosphere and led to the historic Declaration began in the early 1760s at a time when all Americans still considered themselves loyal British subjects. Indeed, in 1763, at the conclusion of the French and Indian War against France, the idea of the colonies breaking free of the mother country was unheard-of, even unthinkable. There was very little separatist feeling in the colonies prior to 1775, the distinguished scholar Samuel E. Morison explains.

> Americans did not start off in 1763 . . . with the conviction that they were entitled to be a separate and independent nation. They never felt . . . that they were so downtrodden by tyrannical masters as to make independence the only solution. On the contrary, Americans were not only content but proud to be part of the British imperium [empire]. But they did feel very strongly that they were entitled to all constitutional rights that Englishmen possessed in England.[9]

Thus, as long as the British government accorded Americans these rights and treated the colonies in a fair and reasonable manner, the colonists appeared content with British rule.

This situation changed rather abruptly when the colonists began to feel that the British king and Parliament were *not* treating them fairly and reasonably. In its victory over France in 1763, Britain gained huge territories in North America, among them southern Canada and

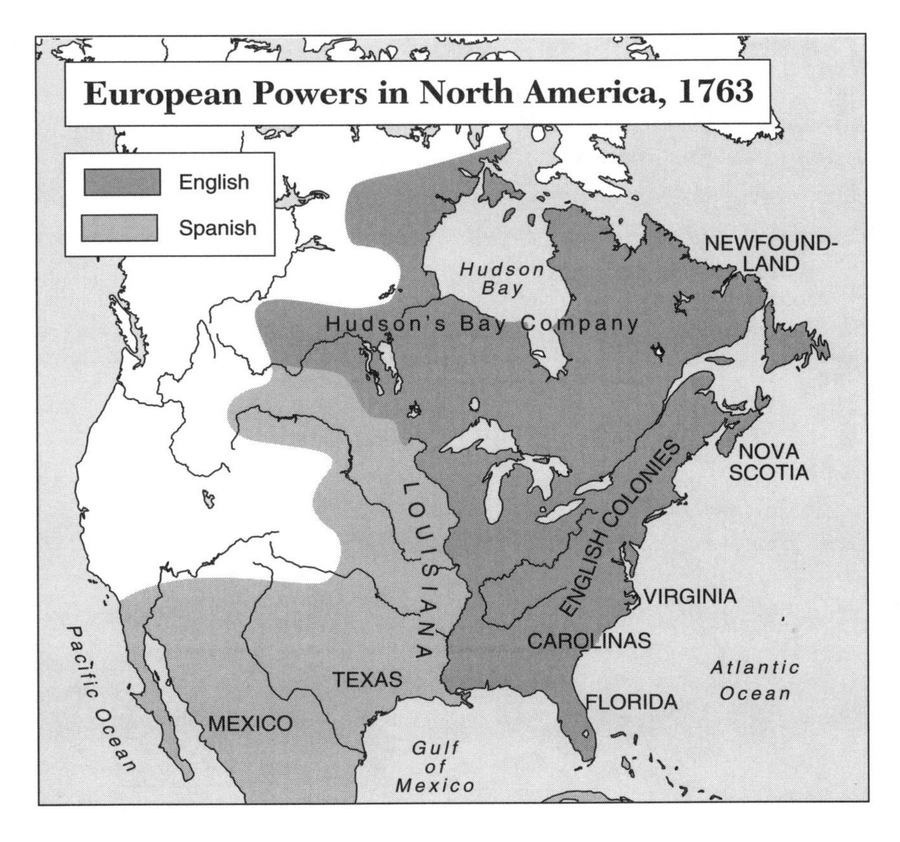

the lands lying between the original thirteen colonies and the Mississippi River. To maintain control over their vast American possessions, especially in the event that France renewed hostilities, the British decided that they needed to keep their army near its wartime strength of eighty-five regiments. The problem was that paying for these troops was a very expensive proposition.

As a partial solution to this problem, the British leadership chose to station large numbers of soldiers in America and to raise the money for their upkeep locally by taxing the colonists. The first such tax was the American Revenue Act of 1764, an altered version of an older customs duty. Foreign sugar and luxury products such as wine, silk, and linen now carried stiff taxes when imported into the American colonies. Several local colonial legislatures objected to the Revenue Act, among them that of New York, which sent a petition to King George III and Parliament claiming it should be exempt from any tax not imposed by its own representatives. "Leave it to the legislative power of the colony," the petition read, "to impose all other [financial] burdens upon its own people, which the public exigencies [needs] may require."[10]

The Stamp Act

Such complaints were mild, however, in comparison to the furor that arose over Parliament's 1765 Stamp Act, the first direct, internal tax Britain had ever imposed on its American colonies. "The Stamp Act," writes historian Harry M. Ward,

> placed duties on paper, vellum [lambskin or calfskin], and parchment to be used for public purposes. . . . All legal and

The British Stamp Act of 1765 declared that all legal and business documents must bear stamps, or raised impressions, like these, certifying payment of the required duty.

An angry colonist makes a speech in a clandestine meeting of the "Sons of Liberty," patriotic Americans opposed to exploitative British taxes.

> business documents, certificates for clearance of ships, court proceedings, pamphlets, newspapers, playing cards, and dice had to be stamped. The stamps were in the form of impressions in relief (like a modern notary seal). The annual burden per colonist would be only about one shilling, equal to one-third of a day's labor. The program would be administered by an American Stamp Office in London; in the colonies there would be one stamp distributor for each of nine districts.[11]

American reactions to the Stamp Act were loud and often violent, as colonists from all walks of life rose in protest. In many cities angry crowds ridiculed and sometimes physically attacked the local citizens chosen to distribute the stamps. In New York, such a crowd broke into the governor's coach house and forced the officer in charge of the stamped paper to burn it, and then marched to the house of another officer, who had promised "to cram the Stamp Act down the people's throats," and ransacked the place. In Boston, irate citizens hanged the local stamp distributor in effigy and destroyed his shop. Afterward, they attacked the homes of royal tax collectors, burning their furniture and tossing their books and personal effects into the streets. Similar unofficial protests, staged by groups of colonists calling themselves the "Sons of Liberty" (often "Liberty Boys"), occurred throughout the American colonies.

Meanwhile, the colonial legislatures unleashed the official protests. The most celebrated was that of Virginia's assembly, the

The Concept of Virtual Representation

The overwhelming majority of British leaders felt that American complaints about "taxation without representation" were groundless, based partly on the argument that the Americans were *represented in Parliament in the "virtual" sense. The members of that distinguished legislature, the argument went, worked diligently and conscientiously to see to the interests and uphold the rights of all English subjects everywhere, including in America. Soame Jenyns, a well-known member of Parliament and the Board of Trade, explained this position in a widely read 1765 pamphlet, saying:*

"That no Englishman is or can be taxed but by his own consent . . . is so far from being true, that it is the very reverse of truth; for no man that I know of is taxed by his own consent, and an Englishman, I believe, is as little likely to be so taxed as any man in the world. . . . Every Englishman is taxed, and not one in twenty represented. . . . Manchester, Birmingham, and many more of our richest and most flourishing trading towns send no members to Parliament . . . because they choose none to represent them; yet are they not Englishmen? or are they not taxed? . . . Why does not this imaginary [virtual] representation extend to America as well as over the whole island of Great Britain? If it can travel three hundred miles, why not three thousand? If it can jump over rivers and mountains, why cannot it sail over the ocean? If the towns of Manchester and Birmingham, sending no representatives to Parliament, are notwithstanding there represented, why are not the cities of Albany and Boston equally represented in that assembly? Are they not alike British subjects? are they not Englishmen? or are they only Englishmen when they solicit for protection, but not Englishmen when taxes are required to enable this country to protect them?"

House of Burgesses, spearheaded by the fiercely patriotic Patrick Henry, which resolved that Virginians were not bound to pay any taxes imposed from outside the colony and that anyone advocating such taxes would be considered an enemy of Virginia. These fiery resolves were published in newspapers all over the colonies; they helped to inspire representatives from nine of the colonies to meet in the so-called "Stamp Act Congress," the first spontaneous expression of colonial unity. In October 1765, this body strongly urged Parliament to repeal the Stamp Act.

Some British leaders agreed with Henry and other angry Americans that the Stamp Act was unjust because the colonists had no representatives in Parliament, the body that had imposed the tax. As cries of "no taxation without representation" rose in America, in January 1766 William Pitt, earl of Chatham, stood before his colleagues in Parliament and urged that the act be repealed. "The Commons of America," he said,

> represented by their several assemblies, have ever been in the possession of the exercise of this, their constitutional right, of giving and granting their own money. They would have been slaves if they had not enjoyed it. At the same time, this kingdom . . . has always bound the colonies by her laws, by her regulations, and restrictions in trade, in navigation, in manufactures, in everything, except that of taking their money out of their pockets without their consent.[12]

"We Cannot Be Happy Without Being Free"

Pitt and his followers eventually prevailed and Parliament repealed the Stamp Act in March 1766. But it did so because a majority of its members felt that the act could not be effectively enforced without resorting to major military force, not because of concerns that the colonists had no representation in the British legislature. Whatever the reasoning behind the repeal, the Americans were ecstatic. Celebrations erupted across the land, many of them expressing renewed feelings of loyalty to Britain. New York's assembly voted for erecting a statue of George III and many grateful cities and towns set up busts of William Pitt. To the colonists, the repeal seemed to confirm that the mother country was willing to treat them, her loyal subjects, fairly and reasonably after all.

William Pitt, one of Britain's most distinguished eighteenth-century legislators, often sympathized with the American cause.

But this optimistic mood soon began to fade. The reality was that Britain still badly needed funds to support its colonial regiments. Responding to this need, in 1767 Charles Townshend, chancellor of the British exchequer (roughly equivalent to today's U.S. secretary of the treasury), proposed new duties on goods imported into the colonies from Britain. Covered were glass, lead, paints, paper, and tea. American reaction to these Townshend Acts was reflected in the attitudes expressed in the twelve *Farmer's Letters* published in colonial newspapers late in 1767 by Philadelphia lawyer John Dickinson. After warning his readers that the Townshend duties were just as outrageous a revenue scheme as the Stamp Act, Dickinson wrote in the twelfth letter:

> Let these truths be indelibly impressed on our minds—that we cannot be happy without being free—that we cannot be free without being secure in our property—that we cannot be secure in our property if without our consent others may . . . take it away—that taxes imposed on us by Parliament do thus take it away—that duties raised for the sole purpose of raising money are taxes—that attempts to lay such duties should be instantly and firmly opposed—that this opposition can never be effectual unless it is the united effort of these provinces.[13]

By calling for the colonies to present a united front against Britain in matters of unfair taxation, Dickinson had resurrected the defiant spirit of the Stamp Act Congress and contributed to a steadily intensifying movement toward federal union that would culminate in the Declaration of Independence and birth of the United States in 1776.

The colonies did mount a united effort to fight the Townshend duties. It took the form of voluntary agreements by merchants to boycott the British goods covered under the acts and the promotion of home industries, wearing American-made clothes, and drinking tea grown in the colonies. The effort eventually worked, for American imports fell by nearly a third, leading Parliament to repeal the Townshend Acts in 1770. The one exception was the tax on imported tea, which the British retained; but since the other taxes had been eliminated, and also because the colonies were now enjoying great economic prosperity, few colonists quibbled.

The Boston Tea Party and Coercive Acts

As in the case of the Stamp Act's repeal, the elimination of the Townshend Acts seemed to return the American colonies to a state of relative normalcy. But the resistance movement sprang back to life when a new crisis, by far the worst yet, gripped America early in 1774. The trouble originated with the retained tax on imported tea, a product many Americans had continued to boycott. In May 1773, Parliament passed an act allowing the British East India Company to bypass Britain and sell its tea directly to the American colonies at a reduced price (since the usual duty charged by British ports was now eliminated). This imposed no new tax on imported tea in America;

however, wary colonial radicals interpreted the move as an attempt to bribe American boycotters into buying the tea and paying the duty. Accordingly, resistance mounted and in three of the four major ports that received tea shipments—New York, Philadelphia, and Charleston—locals halted importation of the tea or sent it back.

The scenario in the fourth port—Boston—was quite different. Local patriots demanded that the colonial governor, Thomas Hutchinson, send the tea ships back. When he refused, on December 16, 1773, a band of Liberty Boys dressed up as Mohawk Indians, marched to the waterfront, and dumped 342 chests of tea into the harbor. There was no violence and no one was injured; and a few days later the *Massachusetts Gazette* reported that after the incident, by now referred to as the "Boston Tea Party," the city of Boston "was very quiet during the whole evening and night following."[14]

This quiet proved to be the lull before the storm, however. King George and most of his subjects in England were outraged at what they saw as a willful and unforgivable destruction of property. Prodded by this outrage, Parliament proceeded to play directly into the hands of the American radicals, who were hoping that the Tea Party would instigate a confrontation with the British. The retaliation took the form of the Coercive (or Intolerable) Acts, passed between March and June 1774. Among these were the Boston Port Act, which closed the port of Boston until such time as the colonists paid for the

One of the many later representations of the December 1773 Boston Tea Party, in which a group of disgruntled colonists dumped imported tea into Boston Harbor.

lost tea; the Massachusetts Government and Administration of Justice Act, which placed harsh restrictions on the powers of local government; and the Quartering Act, which allowed the royal governor to quarter British troops in colonial homes.

Parliament had hoped that the Coercive Acts would isolate Massachusetts and make an example of it, thereby discouraging any further colonial resistance to British policies. But the acts had the complete opposite effect, namely that of galvanizing the colonies in a united stance against what large numbers of Americans saw as clear-cut abuses. News of Boston's plight spread via the communication network of the "committees of correspondence," groups organized earlier to keep all colonies informed about the various American-British crises. In defiance of the blockade, other colonies sent thousands of bushels of corn and wheat and tons of other relief supplies to beleaguered Boston. Meanwhile, on May 17, eighty-nine members of Virginia's House of Burgesses, among them George Washington, Thomas Jefferson, and Patrick Henry, met in the Raleigh Tavern in Williamsburg and declared:

> We are . . . clearly of [the] opinion, that an attack made on one of our sister colonies, to compel submission to arbitrary taxes, is an attack made on all British America, and threatens ruin to the rights of all, unless the united wisdom of the whole be applied. And for this purpose it is recommended to the committee of correspondence, that they communicate, with their several corresponding committees, on the expediency of appointing deputies from the several colonies . . . to meet in general Congress.[15]

The First Continental Congress and Suffolk Resolves

Responding to this call for unity, the members of the committees organized what became known as the First Continental Congress. Meeting in Philadelphia in September 1774, fifty-six delegates from twelve of the thirteen colonies tried to formulate a response to what they viewed as growing threats to American liberty. Clearly, all saw the Boston Tea Party and institution of the retaliatory Coercive Acts as a crucial turning point in relations between the colonies and the mother country.

Yet even as these delegates met, most did not see themselves as extremists or agitators and did not seriously consider the idea of separating from Britain, an attitude shared by most colonists. Some of the delegates, Samuel Adams and Patrick Henry perhaps most promi-

Members of the First Continental Congress congregate outside of Independence Hall in Philadelphia in 1774. They wanted the British to repeal the Coercive Acts, widely viewed in America as unreasonable.

nent among them, were clearly radicals who thought a complete split with the mother country was inevitable. But the majority, referred to at the time as "reconciliationists" (because they hoped to reconcile with Britain), wanted only for Parliament and the king to repeal the Coercive Acts, to stop trying to tax the colonies, and in general to act more reasonably. Moderate patriots like Thomas Jefferson and John Jay of New York desired a fair settlement with Britain and continued to reaffirm their allegiance to the mother country.

One avenue of reconciliation the Congress considered was revising the relationship between Britain and the colonies. On September 28, Joseph Galloway of Pennsylvania introduced his Plan of Union, which proposed to settle the power problem by creating an American version of Parliament. That new body and the older British Parliament should, he suggested, have veto powers over each other in matters pertaining to the American colonies. But though most considered it a worthy idea, the delegates ultimately tabled Galloway's plan, for the mood of the meeting had already taken a more radical turn. In mid-September, Massachusetts patriot Paul Revere had arrived with the stunning news of the Suffolk Resolves, drafted by Joseph Warren and passed on September 9 by a clandestine meeting of towns in the Boston area. These statements, the most brazen yet made by Americans against the British, called for Massachusetts to form its own

Patrick Henry (standing, fourth from left), one of the most radical colonial leaders, makes a point during a session of the First Continental Congress.

government in defiance of the royal governor, recommended a near-total economic boycott of British goods, and urged the people to arm themselves in preparation for possible fighting.

The Continental Congress endorsed the Suffolk Resolves. Even Galloway and the other conservatives went along with them for fear that if they did not, they would appear to be taking the British side. Later, on October 14, the Congress issued its own resolves, stating bluntly that the American colonies were "entitled to life, liberty, and property, and that they have never ceded to any sovereign power whatever a right to dispose of either without their consent." The Congress also listed all of the acts passed by the British since 1763 that it deemed offensive and illegal and demanded their repeal. Nevertheless, the document in no way threatened separation from Britain and even held out hope for eventual reconciliation, concluding that the delegates hoped "that their fellow-subjects in Great Britain will . . . restore us to that state in which both countries found happiness and prosperity."[16]

The Point of No Return

But in fact, that so-called happy state between Britain and its colonies was by now shattered and beyond repair. Following the advice of the Suffolk Resolves, many American colonists began arming themselves. In April 1775, the new governor of Massachusetts, General Thomas Gage, learned that patriots had stored a cache of arms in the village of Concord, twenty-one miles west of Boston, and he decided to send troops to destroy these weapons. During the night of April 18, about seven hundred British soldiers set out for Concord. The next morning they found a force of some eighty armed colonial militiamen waiting for them on the town green of the village of Lexington. The British commander called on the colonials to throw down their weapons; but in the heat of the moment shots rang out (the question of which side fired first remains unanswered), and ten minutes later eight Americans lay dead on the green.

The British arrived at Concord at about 8 A.M. There they skirmished with armed colonials at North Bridge, about a mile from the village green, after which more militiamen from surrounding towns steadily converged on the area, their numbers eventually swelling to over four thousand. The odds now clearly against them, at about noon the British decided to retreat. As they marched along, the militiamen followed, sniping at them almost continuously from behind rocks and trees. By the time they reached Boston, the British had lost 73 men killed, 174 wounded, and 26 missing, while the American casualties were 50 killed and 34 wounded.

This day-long exchange of gunfire and bloodletting proved to be the point of no return in British-American relations. As radical revolutionary philosopher Thomas Paine bluntly asserted:

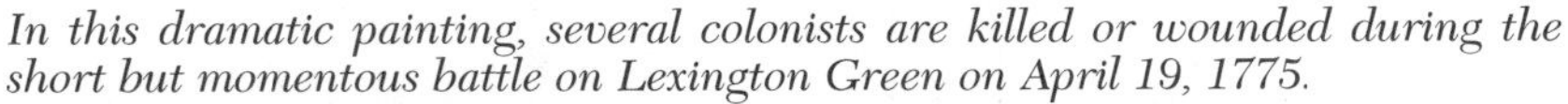

In this dramatic painting, several colonists are killed or wounded during the short but momentous battle on Lexington Green on April 19, 1775.

> All plans, proposals, etc. prior to the nineteenth of April, *i.e.* to the commencement of hostilities, are like the almanacs of the last year; which though proper then . . . are useless now. . . . The independence of America should have been considered as dating its era from . . . *the first musket that was fired against her.*[17]

However apt or poetic this statement may have been at the time, posterity came to view the fighting at Concord and Lexington more specifically as the opening salvo of the Revolutionary War. Official

"'Tis Time to Part"

Perhaps no other American patriot stated the radical colonial position more clearly, ably, and bluntly than Thomas Paine in his 1776 pamphlet, Common Sense. *In these excerpts, he calls for separation from the mother country and criticizes those holding out for reconciliation.*

"Everything that is right or reasonable pleads for separation. The blood of the slain, the weeping voice of nature cries, 'TIS TIME TO PART. Even the distance at which the Almighty hath placed England and America is a strong and natural proof that the authority of the one over the other, was never the design of heaven. . . . Though I would carefully avoid giving unnecessary offense, yet I am inclined to believe, that all those who espouse the doctrine of reconciliation, may be included within the following descriptions. Interested men, who are not to be trusted, weak men who *cannot see*, prejudiced men who will not see, and a certain set of moderate men who think better of the European world than it deserves; and this last class, by an ill-judged deliberation, will be the cause of more calamities to this continent than all the other three."

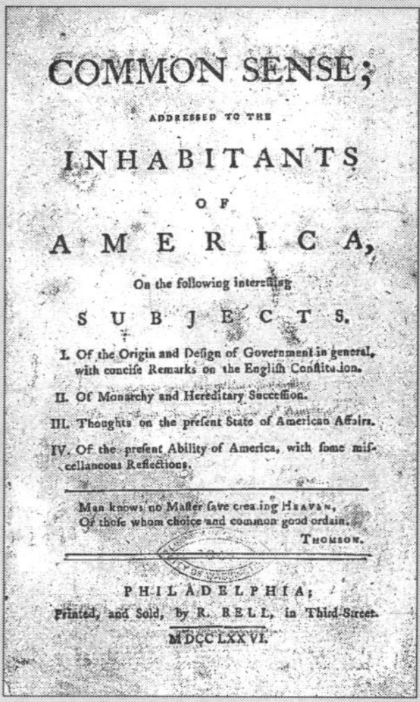

COMMON SENSE;

ADDRESSED TO THE

INHABITANTS

OF

AMERICA,

On the following intereſting

SUBJECTS.

I. Of the Origin and Deſign of Government in general, with conciſe Remarks on the Engliſh Conſtitution.

II. Of Monarchy and Hereditary Succeſſion.

III. Thoughts on the preſent State of American Affairs.

IV. Of the preſent Ability of America, with ſome miſcellaneous Reflections.

Man knows no Maſter ſave creating HEAVEN,
Or thoſe whom choice and common good ordain.
THOMSON.

PHILADELPHIA;
Printed, and Sold, by R. BELL, in Third-Street.
MDCCLXXVI.

The cover page of Thomas Paine's pamphlet Common Sense, *which powerfully challenged Britain's authority over its American colonies.*

Colonial militiamen hurry off to fight the British. The Americans and British fought intermittently for over a year before Congress finally issued the Declaration of Independence.

American independence came over a year later, when the leading patriots approved the July 1776 Declaration, the world's first and perhaps greatest modern governmental statement of human rights. As he composed and placed his name on the document, Jefferson knew that the world into which he had been born was undergoing sweeping and permanent change. But he could scarcely have realized how immense in scope and duration the revolution in human freedom and happiness that he and his colleagues had set in motion would become. Today, after more than two tumultuous centuries, that revolution continues unabated.

The Declaration's Composition and Initial Revision

In 1781, five years after he had written the Declaration of Independence and while he was serving as governor of Virginia, Thomas Jefferson explained to a visiting Indian chief the causes of the American Revolution in the following words:

> You find us, brother, engaged in a war with a powerful nation. Our forefathers were Englishmen, inhabitants of a little island beyond the great water, and, being distressed for land, they came and settled here. As long as we were young and weak, the English . . . made us carry all our wealth to their country, to enrich them; and, not satisfied with this, they at length began to say we . . . should do whatever they ordered us. We were now grown up and felt ourselves strong; we knew we were [as] free as they . . . and we were determined to be free as long as we should exist. For this reason they made war on us.[18]

This version of the events was, of course, vastly oversimplified. Avoiding specifics, Jefferson had left out not only the Stamp and Townshend Acts and the battles at Concord and Lexington, but also the crucial events immediately preceding the Declaration of Independence. Among these was the so-called Olive Branch Petition, pushed through the Continental Congress by moderate patriots John Jay and John Dickinson on July 8, 1775. This document was a last-ditch effort to avert all-out war by asking the king, George III, to hear and consider American grievances about the "tyranny" of Parliament. But the king refused to receive the petition.

The slim American hopes for reconciliation grew even slimmer when, in early November, the news arrived that on August 23 the king had issued a proclamation declaring the colonies to be in a state of open rebellion. Further, American leaders learned, the British were planning to hire German mercenaries to fight the rebels. Adding fuel to the fire, Thomas Paine's pamphlet, *Common Sense*, which vehemently called for separation from Britain, was published in January 1776 and became an instant popular hit, convincing many still-undecided Americans that independence was inevitable. During the spring, radical patriots gained control of most of the colonial legislatures, culminating in the passage of a resolution endorsing independence in the Virginia legislature on May 15. Five days later, John Adams penned his now famous remark summarizing the escalating tensions and discords between the Americans and British: "Every post [mail delivery] and every day rolls in upon us Independence like a torrent."[19] That onrushing tide would soon crash on the shores of a bold new nation.

The King Declares the American Colonists Rebels

Following are excerpts from the August 23, 1775, proclamation issued by George III, in which he officially declared that Britain's American colonies were in a state of rebellion.

"Whereas many of our subjects in divers[e] parts of our Colonies and Plantations in North America, misled by dangerous and ill-designing men, and forgetting the allegiance which they owe to the power that has protected and supported them; after various disorderly acts committed in disturbance of the public peace, to the obstruction of lawful commerce, and to the oppression of our loyal subjects carrying on the same; have at length proceeded to open and avowed rebellion, by arraying themselves in a hostile manner . . . and traitorously preparing, ordering, and levying war against us . . . we have thought fit . . . to issue our Royal Proclamation, hereby declaring, that not only all our Officers, civil and military, are obliged to exert their utmost endeavors to suppress such rebellion, and to bring the traitors to justice, but that all our subjects of this Realm, and the dominions there belonging, are bound by law to be aiding and assisting in the suppression of such rebellion, and to disclose and make known all traitorous conspiracies and attempts against us, our crown and dignity; and we do accordingly strictly charge and command all our Officers . . . and all others [of] our obedient and loyal subjects . . . to make known all treasons . . . and for that purpose, that they transmit to one of our principal Secretaries of State, or other proper officer, due and full information of all persons . . . now in open arms and rebellion against our government."

King George III (1738–1820), who ascended the British throne in 1760, viewed the American patriots as upstarts and rebels who had to be suppressed.

Lee's Resolution on Independence

By early June 1776, most American leaders had committed to the cause of independence and some decided that the next logical step was to draft a congressional resolution that would unite all the colonies in separating from Britain and establishing their own nation. This momentous resolution, proposed on June 7 by Virginia's Richard Henry Lee, was, despite later popular misconceptions, the chief legal organ of American independence. The Declaration of Independence was meant only to implement Lee's resolution by announcing and explaining Congress's fateful action to Britain and the world. At the time, none of the participants could have guessed that posterity would accord the first document relative obscurity and the second immortality.

Richard Henry Lee (1732–1794), who represented Virginia, proposed the June 7, 1776, resolution for independence and later signed the famous Declaration.

In his autobiography, written many years later, Jefferson recalled the introduction of Lee's resolution for independence:

> The delegates from Virginia moved, in obedience to instructions from their constituents, that the Congress should declare that the United colonies are, and of right ought to be, free and independent states, that they are absolved from all allegiance to the British crown, and that all political connection between them and the state of Great Britain is, and ought to be, totally dissolved.[20]

The delegates debated the resolution on June 8 and again on June 10, discussing diverse potential implications of independence. These included the need to effect an alliance with France, which would be instrumental in reducing Britain's transport of war supplies; the importance of opening up trade with other nations to keep Americans adequately supplied during the coming struggle; and the probability that France and Spain would grow jealous of the new American nation, which would pose a threat to their North American possessions.

The upshot of these tense discussions was that some of the delegates were still uneasy about severing all ties with Britain. The principal leaders of the opposition to Lee's resolution, Pennsylvania's

James Wilson and John Dickinson, New York's Robert Livingston, and South Carolina's Edward Rutledge, all claimed personally to favor independence. However, they said, such action might be premature, partly because it was doubtful that America could, at that moment, win a war against Britain; it might be wiser, they argued, to wait until other European countries, including France, had seen the wisdom of supporting American independence as a way of reducing Britain's power. Having thus reached a temporary impasse, the delegates decided to postpone voting on the resolution for a few weeks. During that period, the majority hoped, the uncommitted colonial legislatures would come around and back the measure. As Jefferson remembered it:

> It appearing in the course of these debates, that the colonies of New York, New Jersey, Pennsylvania, Delaware, Maryland, and South Carolina were not yet matured for falling from the parent stem, but that they were fast advancing to that state, it was thought most prudent to wait a while for them, and to postpone the final decision to July 1st.[21]

Choosing the Committee

Those who backed an immediate split with Britain were confident that their still-wavering colleagues would join them. Therefore, to avoid unnecessary delays in the event the resolution passed in early July, the next day, June 11, Congress appointed a committee to draft a declaration to implement the measure. Chosen to write this official announcement of American independence were Jefferson, Adams,

Lee's Call for Independence

This is Richard Henry Lee's threefold resolution of June 7, 1776, calling for independence, the formation of foreign alliances, and a plan for self-government.

"Resolved, that these United Colonies are, and of right ought to be, free and independent states, that they are absolved from all allegiance to the British Crown, and that all political connection between them and the state of Great Britain is and ought to be totally dissolved. That it is expedient forthwith to take the most effectual measures for forming foreign alliances. That a plan of confederation be prepared and transmitted to the respective Colonies for their consideration and approbation [approval]."

and Livingston, along with Benjamin Franklin and Roger Sherman. Livingston (1746–1813), who had practiced law in partnership with his fellow New York delegate, John Jay, before becoming a member of the Continental Congress in 1774, was one of the outstanding legal experts of his time. Sherman (1721–1793), who represented Connecticut in the Congress, had been a county surveyor, state legislator, and superior court judge. Pennsylvania's Franklin (1706–1790), the oldest man in the group, had distinguished himself as a successful newspaper editor and printer and had served as deputy Postmaster General for the colonies (1753–1774). Adams (1735–1826), of Massachusetts, a lawyer known for his intelligence and sharp tongue, had been a major voice in nearly all of Congress's dealings and decisions since being elected to that body in 1774. Jefferson (1743–1826), representing Virginia, had worked briefly as a lawyer in his home state and then served in his state legislature from 1769 to 1774 before joining the Congress in 1775.

A meeting of the drafting committee for the Declaration, including (left to right) Franklin, Jefferson, Adams, Livingston, and Sherman.

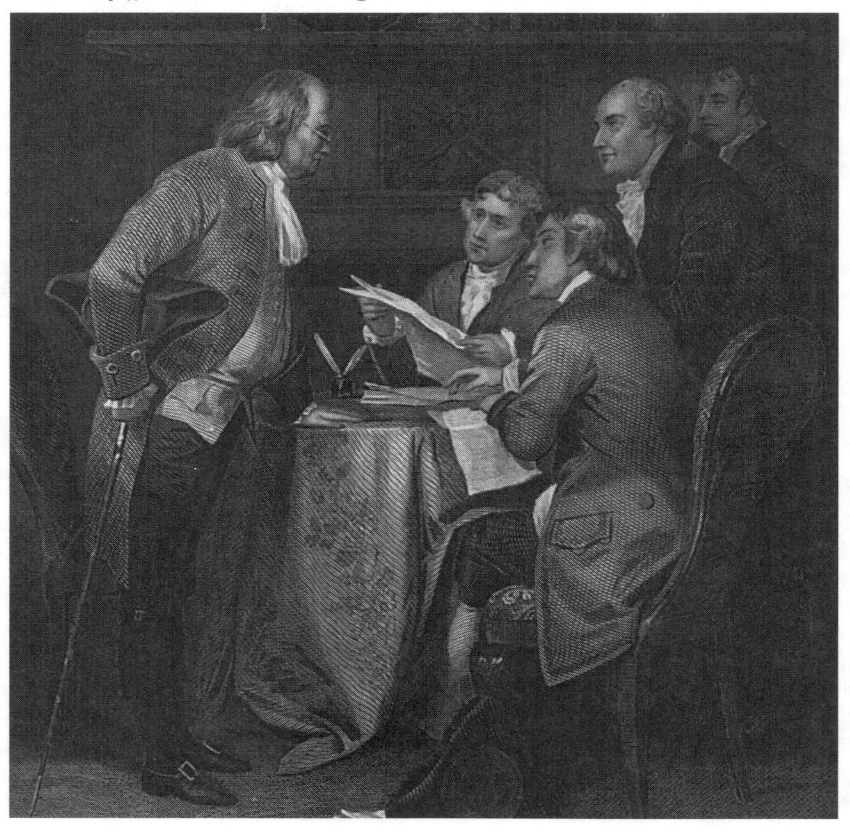

Shortly after having been appointed to the committee, these five men met and briefly discussed the general form that the document should take. Unfortunately, none of them imagined that later generations would be eager to know their every word and gesture, so they kept no notes and the contents of their conversation will never be known. What is certain is that at the end of the session Franklin, Adams, Livingston, and Sherman asked Jefferson to prepare the all-important initial draft.

At first glance, it might seem odd that the committee picked the member who at that moment had the least experience and direct influence in Congress. After all, Jefferson had joined the continental legislature later than the others; moreover, he was not an effective orator and rarely took an active part in legislative debates. From this standpoint, Adams, who *was* a persuasive orator and a frequent leading participant in congressional debates and document-making, would have been a much more logical choice to draft a crucial proclamation. Yet, as biographer Joseph Ellis points out, the fact was "that no one at the time regarded the drafting of the Declaration as a major responsibility or honor," and anyway, the other men were too busy. Adams, for example, was sorely needed to lead the upcoming congressional debate on independence, which was considered a much more crucial task. "Jefferson was asked to draft the Declaration of Independence," Ellis contends, "in great part because the other eligible authors had more important things to do."[22] Another factor at work may have been the seeming appropriateness of assigning the task to a Virginian, since so many of the important revolutionary documents produced thus far had been written by Virginia legislators. What is more, as Dumas Malone and other scholars have suggested, Jefferson was probably considered a better writer than Adams and the others. Adams himself later praised Jefferson's "happy talent of composition" and "felicity [pleasing quality] of expression."[23]

Regrettably, Jefferson's own recollections about why he was chosen to pen the work are not helpful. "The committee for drawing the declaration . . . desired me to do it [and] it was accordingly done," he later wrote without any elaboration.[24] In contrast, Adams provided the following more detailed account, which includes a purported predraft meeting between himself and Jefferson. Historians often question its accuracy, partly because it was written in 1822, some forty-six years later. By that time the Declaration had become renowned and revered, which, they suggest, may have motivated Adams to attempt to make his role in its creation seem larger than it actually was. More importantly, in 1823 Jefferson himself denied that such a meeting ever took place, diplomatically suggesting that his aged colleague had "misremembered." "The committee met," Adams recalled, discussed the subject, and then appointed Mr. Jefferson and me to make the draft, I suppose because we were the two first on the list. The subcommittee [i.e., Adams and Jefferson] met. Jefferson proposed to me to make the draft. I said, "I will not."

"You should do it."

"Oh! no."

"Why will you not? You ought to do it."

"I will not."

"Why?'

"Reason enough."

"What can be your reasons?"

"Reason first—You are a Virginian, and a Virginian ought to appear at the head of this business. Reason second—I am obnoxious, suspected and unpopular. You are very much otherwise. Reason third—You can write ten times better than I can."

"Well," said Jefferson, "if you are decided, I will do as well as I can."[25]

The Creation of the Initial Draft

Because Jefferson never described the actual writing process in any detail, the exact circumstances surrounding his composition of the Declaration's rough draft remain almost as hazy as those concerning his being chosen for the task. However, historians have been able to piece together certain basic facts. First, Jefferson completed the initial work entirely on his own, sometime between June 12 and June 28, 1776, and none of his colleagues had any input until he showed the completed draft to Adams and Franklin toward the end of that period. Jefferson worked in a parlor on the second floor of a house located on the corner of Philadelphia's Seventh and Market Streets. Needing a place to stay during the months in which Congress was meeting to decide the fate of the colonies, he had rented the house from a bricklayer named Jacob Graff. The parlor's now famous folding desk had been built by a Philadelphia cabinetmaker from a design provided by Jefferson himself.[26] It is also fairly certain that Jefferson stood in front of, rather than sat at, the desk as he worked; that he used a goose quill pen (which had to be redipped in an inkwell after every one or two words); and that he labored long hours, often staying up past midnight.

Although it is impossible to know Jefferson's exact state of mind and intentions as he began the rough draft, the form and content of the document reveal his overall purpose and strategy clearly enough. For a format, he chose (or perhaps the committee chose in its initial meeting) a kind of argument called a syllogism, which attempts to persuade the reader or listener by using simple deductive reasoning. The form consists of three parts: a major premise or idea, stated in an introduction; a minor premise, stated and then developed in the body of the work; and finally a conclusion that follows logically from the first two parts. Thus, such an argument states, if premise A and premise B are true, then the conclusion, C, must be the logical and natural result.

Jefferson's purpose was to convince the world that the separation of the colonies from Britain was right and justified. He chose to do this by presenting a moral argument that was at the same time a statement of the daringly democratic political philosophy of the new nation about to be born. For his major premise, therefore, he chose the concept that just governments are established on equal rights and the consent of the governed. "We hold these truths to be sacred and undeniable," the second paragraph of the initial draft began, "that all men are created equal and independent, that from that equal creation they derive rights inherent and inalienable."[27] To make sure these rights are secure, he continued, "governments are instituted among men, deriving their just powers from the consent of the governed"; and if a government denies its citizens these rights, it is the right of said citizens to alter or abolish that government and institute a new, fairer one. The strength of this first premise rested on the fact that it was, as stated, "sacred and undeniable" (which Jefferson changed to "self-evident" in this same initial draft). In other words, it constituted a fundamental human moral truth that needed little or no demonstration; and that made it instantly understandable and appealing to people of reason and good will, no matter what their background or nationality.

This atmospheric engraving shows Jefferson composing the Declaration while standing at the writing desk he had designed himself.

Jefferson's minor premise was that the British king, meaning in effect the British government, had repeatedly threatened and denied the "undeniable" rights of the American colonists. The development

A Declaration by the Representatives of the UNITED STATES OF AMERICA, in General Congress assembled.

When in the course of human events it becomes necessary for one people to dissolve the political bands which have connected them with another, and to assume among the powers of the earth the separate and equal station to which the laws of nature & of nature's god entitle them, a decent respect to the opinions of mankind requires that they should declare the causes which impel them to the separation.

We hold these truths to be self-evident, that all men are created equal; that they are endowed by their creator with certain inherent & inalienable rights; that among these are life, liberty, & the pursuit of happiness; that to secure these rights, governments are instituted among men, deriving their just powers from the consent of the governed; that whenever any form of government

This portion of the front page of one of the early drafts of the Declaration shows deletions and additions made by Jefferson, Franklin, and Adams. Most of the changes made in Jefferson's original version were minor.

of this premise, making up most of the body of the work, took the form of a list of eighteen charges against the king, among them: "He has dissolved representative houses repeatedly and continually for opposing with manly firmness his invasions on the rights of the people"; and "He has kept among us in times of peace standing armies and ships of war without the consent of our legislatures."

The conclusion of Jefferson's argument followed automatically from the two premises he had "proved." Thus, A: just governments do not deny their citizens basic, inherent rights, such as equality, and if they do, citizens have the right to abolish said governments; and B: the British king had repeatedly denied his American subjects their rights as Englishmen; therefore, C: the colonists were justified in renouncing allegiance to Britain and declaring "these colonies to be free and independent states." Furthermore, as free states they had "full power to levy war, conclude peace, contract alliances, establish commerce, and to do all other acts and things which independent states may of right do."

The Early Revisions

After finishing the original draft of the Declaration, Jefferson's next step was to show it to other members of the drafting committee for possible revisions. Again, the exact series of events is unknown. Jefferson's own later recollection was only that before I reported it [the draft] to the committee, I communicated it *separately* to Dr. Franklin and Mr. Adams, requesting their corrections, because they were the two members of whose judgments and amendments I wished most to have the benefit before presenting it to the committee.[28]

The best guess of modern historians is that Jefferson submitted the draft to Franklin and Adams sometime in the days immediately preceding June 28, the date the committee presented a revised draft to Congress.

In this short span of a few days, the three men met, likely at least twice and possibly three or four times, and made a total of twenty-six changes. Twenty-three of these were alterations made in phraseology, or wording, two in Adams's handwriting, five in Franklin's, and sixteen in Jefferson's. The other three changes were additions of new paragraphs, all of them very brief. Carl Becker, one of the leading experts on the Declaration and its creation, suggests the following scenario for this earliest revision process:

> Jefferson first submitted it [the draft] to Franklin. Franklin then wrote in one, and probably two, of the five corrections that appear in his hand. Where the draft read, "and amount of their salaries" [in the charge against the king reading: "He has made our judges dependent on his will alone, for the tenure of their offices, and amount of their salaries."], Franklin changed it to read, "and *the* amount *and payment* of their salaries." A second correction by Franklin was probably

John Adams (1735–1826), at left, and Benjamin Franklin (1706–1790) helped Jefferson revise the Declaration before they presented it to Congress for approval.

> made at this time also. Jefferson originally wrote, "reduce them to arbitrary power" [in the section reading "but when a long train of abuses and usurpations . . . evinces a design to reduce them to arbitrary power, it is their right . . . to throw off such government"]. Franklin's correction reads "reduce them under absolute despotism.". . . At all events, not more than two of Franklin's five corrections had been made when Jefferson submitted the draft to Adams. Adams then wrote in one of his two corrections: where Jefferson had written "for a long space of time" [in the charges against the king reading "He has dissolved representative houses repeatedly. . . . He has refused for a long space of time to cause others to be elected"], Adams added "after such dissolutions." Having made this correction, Adams . . . returned the draft to Jefferson. After receiving the draft from Adams, Jefferson wrote in at least the greater part of the sixteen verbal changes and three new paragraphs. . . . [For example,] Jefferson wrote out on a slip of paper the following paragraph: "He [the king] has called together legislative bodies at places unusual, uncomfortable, and distant from the depository of their public records, for the sole purpose of fatiguing them into compliance with his measures." The slip was then pasted at one end to the rough draft at the place where occurs the paragraph beginning, "he has dissolved representative houses repeatedly and continually."[29]

After making these revisions, Jefferson apparently resubmitted the draft to Franklin and Adams, who made the rest of their few documented early changes. Livingston and Sherman then presumably examined the document and signified their approval. Finally, the committee submitted the revised draft, referred to then and now as the "fair copy," to Congress.

Magical Words and Phrases

The document that Jefferson had produced largely on his own and in the span of little more than ten days went far beyond the original purpose and expectations of the task he had been assigned. More than a simple statement of and list of reasons for a group of colonies to separate from their mother country, the Declaration was a moving and timeless affirmation of human rights and values. Jefferson had been sorely restricted by a set literary format and extremely limited space. Yet in defiance of these restraints, he had dazzlingly demonstrated the "felicity of expression" with which Adams had

Sample Revisions of the Declaration's Initial Draft

Some of the minor alterations the Declaration of Independence underwent during the various stages of revision can be seen in this comparison of the opening sentences as Jefferson first wrote them in Jacob Graff's parlor (presented in italics) with their final form as approved on July 4, 1776. Note the changes in capitalization as well as wording.

"When in the course of human events it becomes necessary for a people to advance from that subordination in which they have hitherto remained, and to assume among the powers of the earth the equal and independent station to which the laws of nature and nature's god entitle them, a decent respect to the opinions of mankind requires that they should declare the causes which impel them to the change.

We hold these truths to be sacred and undeniable; that all men are created equal and independent, that from that equal creation they derive rights inherent and inalienable, among which are the preservation of life, and liberty and the pursuit of happiness; that to secure these ends, governments are instituted among men, deriving their just powers from the consent of the governed; that whenever any form of government shall become destructive of these ends, it is the right of the people to alter or to abolish it, and to institute new government."

"When in the Course of human events, it becomes necessary for one people to dissolve the political bands which have connected them with another, and to assume among the Powers of the earth, the separate and equal station to which the Laws of Nature and of Nature's God entitle them, a decent respect to the opinions of mankind requires that they should declare the causes which impel them to the Separation.

We hold these truths to be self-evident, that all men are created equal, that they are endowed by their Creator with certain unalienable Rights, that among these are Life, Liberty and the Pursuit of Happiness—That to secure these rights, Governments are instituted among Men, deriving their just Powers from the Consent of the Governed. That whenever any Form of Government becomes destructive of these ends, it is the Right of the People to alter or to abolish it, and to institute new Government."

credited him. He had managed to capture most of the core essences of human dignity and democratic theory and to translate these lofty ideas into simple terms that anyone anywhere could readily comprehend.

These terms took the form of several noble and electrifying phrases, one following closely on another, especially in the document's opening and closing paragraphs: "The course of human events," "the laws of nature and of nature's god entitle them," "all men are created equal," "life, liberty and the pursuit of happiness," "just powers from the consent of the governed," "the right of the people," "their safety and happiness," "the voice of justice," "hold them as we hold the rest of mankind," "appealing to the supreme judge of the world," "our lives, our fortunes, our sacred honor." Jefferson seemed innately to grasp that the use of such concise, stirring phrases was the best, perhaps the only effective way to turn a short statement justifying separation from Britain into a universal affirmation of freedom and self-determination. Noted Jefferson biographer Merrill Peterson describes the historic literary feat this way:

> In a document of less than 1500 words, most of it a bill of particulars against a reigning sovereign, ideas could not be developed, nor indeed even stated; they could only be conjured up by magical words and phrases in trim array. Jefferson managed to compress a cosmology [universal or world view], a political philosophy, a national creed in the second paragraph of the declaration. This was a triumph. It raised the American cause above parochialism [narrow, local concerns], above history, and united it with the cause of mankind. A philosophy of human rights attained timeless symbolization in words that inspired action; action became thought and thought became action.[30]

Before any concrete action could be taken, however, Congress had to approve the Declaration. Jefferson and his fellow committee members knew full well, moreover, that neither debate on nor final revision and approval of the document would take place before the delegates had debated and passed Lee's resolution on independence. For if the colonies could not unanimously agree to break away from Britain's grasp, the Declaration would remain only an unpublished rough draft, perhaps to be shoved into a drawer and forgotten. Such a bleak scenario never took place, of course. The debates on the crucial resolution and the document written to implement it *did* take place; and they proved to be among the most interesting and gripping in American history.

Chapter 3
The Enlightened Ideas that Inspired the Declaration

That Thomas Jefferson was chosen by the other members of the drafting committee to write the rough draft for the Declaration of Independence and that he did so between June 12 and 28, 1776, are indisputable facts. Somewhat less certain are the exact sources of the many stirring phrases and ideas that fill the document; although modern scholars do know, with reasonable certainty, the major writers who shaped Jefferson's political philosophy and world view. Speculation about the intellectual forces that inspired the Declaration and other important writings by Jefferson and other founders continues to generate many articles and books each year.

This kind of speculation is far from new. And it may come as a surprise to some that the conclusions drawn from such conjecture have not always been positive and complimentary. When Jefferson was an old man, for instance, some of his former colleagues attempted, for reasons of their own, to downplay and even to belittle his achievement in writing the Declaration. A prominent example was Massachusetts legislator Timothy Pickering, a frequent political opponent of Jefferson's in the early decades of the new nation. The document "contained no new ideas," Pickering charged, and "is a common-place compilation, its sentiments hacknied [frequently discussed] in Congress for two years before."[31] Attempting to rebut such criticisms, Jefferson claimed that he had not directly copied any other documents when drafting the Declaration. "I turned to neither book nor pamphlet while writing it," he stated in 1823;[32] and historians generally agree with this claim.

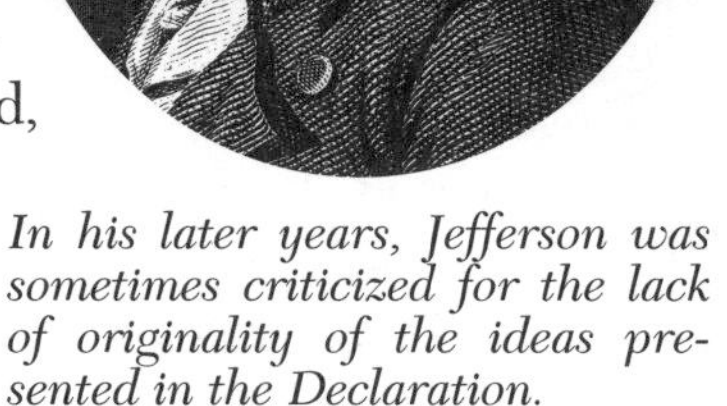

In his later years, Jefferson was sometimes criticized for the lack of originality of the ideas presented in the Declaration.

Yet, though overly harsh and dismissive of what was undoubtedly a superlative job of writing, Pickering's charge that the document contained few, if any, original ideas was in essence true. The fact was that Jefferson, like other educated Americans of his day, was a product of the European political and intellectual currents of the seventeenth and eighteenth centuries. And it was only natural that he would draw on the ideas of the philosophers (especially English and French ones) who had shaped these currents, as well as earlier thinkers who had influenced said philosophers. In fact, these ideas were "so deeply imbedded in the thinking of educated Americans of the period that they came to mind unbidden," states former Harvard University scholar Carl Friedrich.[33] Biographer Merrill Peterson agrees, writing that "the ideas in the Declaration belonged to everyone and to no one. They were part of the climate of opinion, and they passed as coin of the realm among American patriots in 1776."[34] Jefferson himself expressed the same sentiment:

> I did not consider it as any part of my charge to invent new ideas altogether, and to offer no sentiment which had ever been expressed before. . . . Neither aiming at originality of principle or sentiment, nor yet copied from any particular and previous writing, it was intended to be an expression of the American mind, and to give to that expression the proper tone and spirit called for by the occasion.[35]

Thus, the fact that Jefferson's ideas were not original does not in any way detract from his talent and unique achievement in writing the Declaration. It was the special way that he combined and stated those ideas, making them strikingly relevant to the colonial situation of 1775–1776, that makes the document great.

Borrowed Words and Phrases

The content of the Declaration of Independence, like that of most other such documents, consists of two elements: the specific words and phrases used and the ideas those words and phrases are intended to convey. Regarding the first element, there is no doubt that Jefferson did borrow some individual words, phrases, and even whole sentences from his own earlier writings. The principal example is the preamble he had written for the new constitution for his native state in May 1776, only weeks before beginning work on the Declaration. (As he composed various drafts in Philadelphia, couriers carried them to Williamsburg, then Virginia's capital, where the Virginia legislators were meeting.) The preamble contained a list of grievances against George III. The similarities between this list and the one in the Declaration are illustrated in the following comparison of key phrases from the two documents (with those from the preamble shown in italics):

Whereas George the Third . . . hath endeavored to pervert [his office] into a detestable and unsupportable tyranny . . .
The history of the present king of Great Britain is a history of repeated injuries . . . all having in direct object the establishment of a tyranny . . .

By putting his negative on laws the most wholesome and necessary for the public good . . .
He has refused his assent to laws the most wholesome and necessary to the public good.

By denying his governors permission to pass laws of immediate and pressing importance, unless suspended in their operation for his assent, and, when so suspended, neglecting to attend to them for many years . . .
He has forbidden his governors to pass laws of immediate and pressing importance, unless suspended in their operation till his assent shall be obtained; and, when so suspended, he has utterly neglected to attend to them.

By plundering our seas, ravaging our coasts, burning our towns, and destroying the lives of our people . . .
He has plundered our seas, ravaged our coasts, burnt our towns, and destroyed the lives of our people.[36]

That Jefferson used substantially the same list in both documents is neither surprising nor improper. It is likely that he and his colleagues on the drafting committee decided in their preliminary meeting that the Declaration should include such a list of charges; and they may even have agreed beforehand that these charges should cover the same ground as those he had compiled for the Virginia constitution.

Since, in transferring parts of this list of grievances from one document to the other, Jefferson was quoting his own words, which had been written shortly before, he can hardly be accused of copying someone else in this instance. However, over the centuries he *has* been accused from time to time of copying other words and phrases in the Declaration, most often from Virginia legislator George Mason. In fact, while Jefferson was working on the preamble for the Virginia constitution, Mason was drafting a bill of rights for the same document. Comparing the first article of Mason's bill to the opening of the second paragraph of Jefferson's first draft of the Declaration, similarities are certainly obvious:

Mason: That all men are by nature equally free and independent, and have certain inherent rights . . . namely, the

VIRGINIA BILL *of* RIGHTS

DRAWN ORIGINALLY BY GEORGE MASON AND
ADOPTED BY THE CONVENTION OF DELEGATES

June 12, 1776.

A Declaration of Rights made by the Repreſentatives of the good People of Virginia, aſſembled in full and free Convention; which Rights do pertain to them, and their Poſterity, as the Baſis and Foundation of Government.

I.

That all Men are by Nature equally free and independent, and have certain inherent Rights, of which, when they enter into a State of Society, they cannot, by any Compact, deprive or diveſt their Poſterity; namely, the Enjoyment of Life and Liberty, with the Means of acquiring and poſſeſſing Property, and purſuing and obtaining Happineſs and Safety.

II.

That all Power is veſted in, and conſequently derived from, the People; that Magiſtrates are their Truſtees and Servants, and at all Times amenable to them.

III.

That Government is, or ought to be, inſtituted for the common Benefit, Protection, and Security, of the People, Nation, or Community; of all the various Modes and Forms of Government that is beſt, which is capable of producing the greateſt Degree of Happineſs and Safety, and is moſt effectually ſecured againſt the Danger of Mal-adminiſtration; and that, whenever any Government ſhall be found inadequate or contrary to theſe Purpoſes, a Majority of the Community hath an indubitable, unalienable, and indefeaſible Right, to reform, alter, or aboliſh it, in ſuch Manner as ſhall be judged moſt conducive to the public Weal.

IV.

That no Man, or Set of Men, are entitled to excluſive or ſeparate Emoluments or Privileges from the Community, but in Conſideration of public Services; which, not being deſcendible, neither ought the Offices of Magiſtrate, Legiſlator, or Judge, to be hereditary.

V.

That the legiſlative and executive Powers of the State ſhould be ſeparate and diſtinct from the Judicative; and, that the Members of the two firſt may be reſtrained from Oppreſſion, by feeling and participating the Burthens of the People, they ſhould, at fixed Periods, be reduced to a private Station, return into that Body from which they were originally taken, and the Vacancies be ſupplied by frequent, certain, and regular Elections, in which all, or any Part of the former Members, to be again eligible, or ineligible, as the Laws ſhall direct.

That

The first page of Virginia's bill of rights, drafted by George Mason.

enjoyment of life and liberty, with the means of acquiring and possessing property, and pursuing and obtaining happiness and safety.

Jefferson: That all men are created equal and independent; that from that equal creation they derive rights inherent and inalienable, among which are the preservation of life, and liberty, and the pursuit of happiness.[37]

There is no dispute about whose document came first. On June 12, 1776, the day the Virginia legislature adopted Mason's bill, the *Pennsylvania Gazette* published the document and there is little doubt that Jefferson, then in Philadelphia, read it just as he was beginning work on the Declaration. So it is feasible that Jefferson borrowed some words from Mason, most probably "life," "liberty," "pursue," and "happiness"; and if so, Jefferson regrouped them into a more concise and powerful phrase. But this does not mean that Jefferson could not think of what to write on his own and had to copy Mason. The reality is that most of these words, as well as the ideas behind them, were not original with either Mason *or* Jefferson, but came from an earlier and common source intimately familiar to all of the American founders. As Joseph Ellis puts it, although Jefferson may

George Mason on Freedom, Happiness, and Fair Government

These excerpts from the Virginia Bill of Rights, *drafted by George Mason and adopted on June 12, 1776, reflect the ideals and language of the Enlightenment, the liberal European intellectual movement that also inspired Jefferson's writings, including the Declaration of Independence.*

"1. That all men are by nature equally free and independent, and have certain inherent rights, of which, when they enter into a state of society, they cannot, by any compact, deprive or divest their posterity; namely, the enjoyment of life and liberty, with the means of acquiring and possessing property, and pursuing and obtaining happiness and safety.

2. That all power is vested in, and consequently derived from, the people; that magistrates [public officials] are their trustees and servants, and at all times amenable to them.

3. That government is, and ought to be, instituted for the common benefit, protection, and security, of the people, nation, or community; of all the various modes and forms of government, that [one] is best which is capable of producing the greatest degree of happiness and safety . . . and that whenever any government shall be found inadequate or contrary to these purposes, a majority of the community hath an . . . inalienable . . . right, to reform, alter, or abolish it. . . .

5. That the legislative and executive powers of the state should be separate and distinct from the judicative [judiciary]. . . .

6. That elections of members to serve as representatives of the people, in assembly, ought to be free. . . .

12. That the freedom of the press is one of the great bulwarks of liberty, and can never be restrained but by despotic governments."

have borrowed some specific language from Mason, "both men knew whom they were paraphrasing."[38] The "whom" in this case was the seventeenth-century English philosopher, John Locke.

The Enlightenment and Natural Law

Locke (1632–1704), the political theorist who influenced the American patriots more than any other thinker, was a staunch advocate of civil and religious liberties. As such, he was one of the major figures of the great seventeenth- and eighteenth-century intellectual movement usually referred to as the European Enlightenment. Spearheaded mainly by liberal English and French thinkers, the Enlightenment was characterized by its appeal to and celebration of human reason, newly discovered scientific facts, religious toleration, the existence of certain basic natural human rights, and fair government. Enlightenment philosophers held that science might reveal the true nature of the world, which humans could then, in essence remake, controlling and exploiting it to their advantage. Part of this rebirth, they suggested, was a new understanding of human nature, emphasizing certain inherent rights, including freedom of thought, the right of self-expression, and individual personal fulfillment.

The Enlightenment thinkers did not claim to have invented these ideas about natural law and natural human rights. Rather, they saw themselves as rediscovering, and then building on and in a sense *re*-inventing, certain concepts that had been introduced by venerable ancient Greek and Roman writers and subsequently lost. The fourth-century B.C. Greek philosopher Aristotle, for instance, spoke of the existence of "natural" justice in his *Nicomachean Ethics*, saying that

> there are two sorts of political justice, one natural and the other legal. The natural is that which has the same validity everywhere and does not depend upon acceptance [in any specific place or time]; the legal is that which . . . once laid down, is decisive, [for example] that . . . a goat shall be sacrificed and not two sheep. . . . Some hold the view that all regulations are of this kind, on the ground that whereas natural laws are immutable [unchangeable] and have the same validity everywhere (as fire burns both here and in Persia), they can see the notions of justice are variable . . . but still, some things are so by nature and some are not.[39]

Later, some Roman thinkers developed this idea of ethical and rational laws of nature, among them the great first-century B.C. orator and statesman, Cicero. In his *Republic*, he argued that such laws are applicable to people in all societies:

True law is, indeed, right reason, comfortable to nature, pervading all things, constant, eternal. . . . It is not lawful to alter this law, to derogate from it, or to repeal it. Nor can we possibly be absolved from this law, either by the Senate or the people . . . nor will it be one law for Rome and another for Athens; one thing today and another tomorrow; but it is a law eternal and unchangeable for all people and in every age.[40]

That this truly noble sentiment is so strikingly similar to Abraham Lincoln's appraisal of the Declaration of Independence as "applicable to all men and all times" is not as surprising as it might seem. The Declaration's author, Jefferson, was familiar with both Aristotle's and Cicero's writings and ideas. And he was equally steeped in the theories of Locke and other Enlightenment thinkers who had developed these ancient ideas and applied them to a more modern political and social context. Indeed, throughout the 1600s and 1700s, the Enlightenment's liberal theories slowly, but steadily and profoundly, transformed the way that educated people in Europe and America viewed certain political and social institutions that had been taken for granted for many centuries.

Imprinted With Locke's Doctrines

For example, Locke, like many other Enlightenment thinkers, argued that traditional societies ruled by absolute monarchs tended to stifle people's natural inherent rights. In various works that were widely read in Europe and America, particularly his epic *Two Treatises of Government* (1690), he denied the divine right of kings, stating that government should be based on the consent of the governed. Indeed, said Locke, the very function of government should be to preserve people's natural, or God-given, rights; and among these, are life, liberty, and property. "We must consider what state all men are naturally in," Locke states in his second treatise,

John Locke, the seventeenth-century English philosopher who inspired the American patriots.

and that is a state of perfect freedom to order their actions and dispose of their possessions . . . as they think fit, within the bounds of the law of nature, without asking leave or depending upon the will of any other man. . . . And reason, which is that law, teaches all mankind . . . that, being equal and independent, no one ought to harm another in his life, health, liberty or possessions.[41]

This and other similar statements by Locke, therefore, constituted the major source of the American founders' fervent convictions about natural law and the natural rights they believed were the birthright of all persons. Clearly, Locke was also the inspiration for both Jefferson's and Mason's frequent use of the words "life," "liberty," "property," and "free and independent."

Jefferson's statement in the Declaration that, when a government becomes destructive "it is the right of the people to alter or abolish it," a belief shared by his colleagues, was also inspired principally by Locke. When rulers threaten or violate the people's rights, Locke maintained, the people have the right to rise up and "oppose" those rulers. "The end of government is the good of mankind," he writes.

John Locke Defines Natural Law and Natural Rights

This seminal statement of God-given human rights comes from chapter 2 of Locke's Second Treatise of Government.

"To understand political power . . . we must consider what state all men are naturally in, and that is a state of perfect freedom to order their actions and dispose of their possessions . . . as they think fit, within the bounds of the law of nature, without asking leave or depending upon the will of any other man. . . . A state also of equality [is one] wherein all the power and jurisdiction is reciprocal [shared by all], no one having more than another; there being nothing more evident than that creatures of the same species and rank . . . should also be equal one amongst another without subordination or subjection [i.e., inferior status or servitude]. . . . But though this be a state of liberty, yet it is not a state of license. . . . The state of nature has a law of nature to govern it, which obliges everyone; and reason, which is that law, teaches all mankind . . . that, being equal and independent, no one ought to harm another in his life, health, liberty or possession. . . . And that all men may be restrained from invading others' rights and from doing hurt to one another, and the law of nature be observed, which wills the peace and preservation of all mankind, the execution of the law of nature is, in that state, put into every man's hands. . . . In transgressing the law of nature, the offender declares himself to live by another rule than that of reason and common equity; which is that measure God has set to the actions of men for their mutual security."

> And which is best for mankind? That the people should be always exposed to the boundless will of tyranny, or that the rulers should be sometimes liable to be opposed when they grow exorbitant [excessive] in the use of their power and employ it for the destruction and not the preservation of the properties of their people?[42]

It must be emphasized that, while Jefferson, Mason, and other American founders regularly spouted words and ideas popularized by Locke, they did not consciously attempt to copy him. Again, Locke's ideas were not new. Copies of his books had circulated through the American colonies for many years; his political and moral concepts were widely used as the basis for sermons by American clergymen, especially after 1763. By the 1770s, Locke's ideas had become so ingrained in men like Jefferson that they tended to draw on them automatically when the situation called for it. In fact, scholar Samuel E. Morison suggests, the principles and language of Locke's second treatise were so much a part of Jefferson's mind that "unconsciously he thought and wrote like Locke."[43] And because Jefferson and the other men who created the United States were so imprinted with Locke's doctrines, these doctrines became a permanent part of the fabric of the new nation. "Locke's individualism, his glorification of property rights and his love of conscience," states noted scholar Paschal Larkin, "have been interwoven into the economic and social texture of American life."[44]

Montesquieu and the Separation of Powers

Of course, Locke was not the only Enlightenment thinker who influenced the American patriots in formulating the Declaration of Independence and other fundamental documents of their new and unprecedentedly democratic nation. Another was the great French political philosopher, historian, and jurist, Charles de Montesquieu (1689–1755). Montesquieu himself had felt the influence of Locke. Like the American founders did later, the Frenchman heard and heeded Locke's argument that, in order to restrain the excesses of tyrannical government, the people should "balance" government power by "placing several parts of it in different hands."[45] Locke did not fully develop the concept of separation of governmental powers, however. He held that there are three functions of government—legislative, executive, and federative (dealing with foreign relations). In Locke's mind, England already had an effective legislature that fairly represented the people, namely Parliament; while he was content to allow the British king to handle both executive and federative functions as long as the monarch did not abuse his powers.

Montesquieu carried the concept of separation of powers an important step further, stating in his 1748 masterwork, *The Spirit of the Laws*, that a just government must be divided into three fully independent parts, the legislative, executive, and judicial. He wrote:

> When legislative power is united with executive power in a single person or in a single body of the magistracy, there is no liberty, because one can fear that the same monarch or senate that makes tyrannical laws will execute them tyrannically. Nor is there liberty if the power of judging is not separate from legislative power and from executive power. If it were joined to legislative power, the power over the life and liberty of the citizens would be arbitrary [subject to the whims of the powerful], for the judge would be the legislator. If it were joined to executive power, the judge could have the force of an oppressor. All would be lost if the same man or the same body of principal men . . . exercised these three powers, that of making laws, that of executing public resolutions, and that of judging the crimes or the disputes of individuals.[46]

Montesquieu was one of the leading political philosophers of the Enlightenment.

Jefferson did not explicitly refer to such separation of powers in the Declaration, since this document was meant to be only a brief rationale for separation from Britain. The concept is nevertheless *implicit* in the text. Jefferson and his colleagues were well aware of Montesquieu's ideas, which they held in the highest regard. Moreover, knowing that they would soon have to formulate a government for the new nation they were creating, many of them were already contemplating using the Frenchman's three-fold breakdown of powers. This is proven by the fifth article of Mason's Virginia rights bill, which advocated just such a breakdown. And Jefferson certainly had the same ideas in mind when he penned these sentences in the Declaration's second paragraph:

> Whenever any form of government becomes destructive . . . it is the right of the people to alter or to abolish it, and to institute new government, *laying its foundation on such principles, and organizing its powers in such form, as to them shall seem most likely to effect their safety and happiness* [emphasis added].[47]

The phrase, "organizing its powers in such form," was a clear reference to the ideas developed by Montesquieu and advocated by Mason; it was an equally clear signal to the world that the American founders intended to implement these ideas. Advocacy of the doctrine of separation of powers was also implicit later in the Declaration, in Jefferson's list of grievances against the king. By citing and condemning the king's abuses of power, he was justifying and laying the groundwork for the creation of a government in which no single person or group could amass and abuse great power.

The Enlightenment's American Branch

In addition to Locke's and Montesquieu's ideas, the American patriots were familiar with and drew on those of other Enlightenment thinkers. Among these were English philosopher and essayist Francis Bacon (1561–1626); English mathematician and natural philosopher Isaac Newton (1642–1727); English/Scottish philosopher Francis Hutcheson (1694–1746); English political theorist Algernon Sidney (1622–1683); and the French philosophers, Voltaire (François Marie Arouet, 1694–1778), and Jean Jacques Rousseau (1712–1778). Yet it would be misleading and a decided disservice to Jefferson and his colleagues to suggest that the liberal climate of opinion these European thinkers created in eighteenth-century America constituted the sum total of American intellectual endeavor. Indeed, most American leaders were highly educated and some were gifted thinkers and writers in their own right. Not infrequently, they took the ideas of Locke, Montesquieu, and others and translated them brilliantly into terms that fit their own particular colonial situation. And it would not be an exaggeration to say that Jefferson, Franklin, and a handful of other American intellectuals of the day were the proponents of a new, American offshoot of the Enlightenment.

The case of Jefferson and the Declaration of Independence is a perfect example. Although filled with language and ideas drawn from Locke and others, the document unquestionably bears the stamp of his own individuality and genius. The vision that Jefferson captured in the natural rights portion of the Declaration, biographer Joseph Ellis suggests, represented a special

> formulation of the Jeffersonian imagination. The specific form of the vision undoubtedly drew upon language Locke had used. . . . But the urge to embrace such an ideal society came from deep within Jefferson himself. It was the vision of a young man projecting his personal cravings for a world in which all behavior was voluntary and therefore all coercion unnecessary, where independence and equality never collided. . . . Though

> indebted to Locke, Jefferson's political vision was more radical . . . driven as it was by a youthful romanticism unwilling to negotiate its high standards with an imperfect world. . . . Jefferson provided a sanction for youthful hopes and illusions, planted squarely in what turned out to be the founding document of the American republic. The American dream, then, is . . . the Jeffersonian dream writ [written] large.[48]

In other words, the achievement of Jefferson and his colleagues was to take the Enlightenment's intellectual conjectures about equality and fair government and to turn them into realistic and immediate objectives. The American patriots transformed Locke's ideas into action to a degree and on a scale that he never imagined possible. In documents like the Declaration and his earlier *Notes on Virginia*, for instance, Jefferson created what has been called an agenda for the American branch of the Enlightenment, which was more radical and uncompromising than its European counterpart. It was an agenda, writes historian Henry Commager, that,

> though it drew its inspiration from the Old World Enlightenment, inevitably differed from it. It relied on reason, it rejoiced in freedom, it embraced humanitarianism, it was confident of progress, and—here the difference is dramatic—it was able, as the Old World was not, to translate these principles and faiths into [real] practices and institutions.[49]

A Practical Vision of Human Happiness

One of the most powerful illustrations of the way the American founders translated Old World ideas into New World realities was their almost reverent invocation of the "right" to happiness. European Enlightenment thinkers often mentioned the people's happiness as one of the ideal goals of government. American political and social theorists and writers embraced this concept enthusiastically. George Mason inserted it into Virginia's bill of rights; John Adams mentioned it no less than five times in the constitution he drafted for his home state of Massachusetts; and numerous American patriots, from Thomas Paine to George Washington, invoked it repeatedly in letters and speeches. The most famous reference to the right to happiness, of course, was Jefferson's. All people are endowed, the Declaration of Independence states, with the rights of "life, liberty, and the pursuit of happiness."

But there was an important difference between the way European writers envisioned the natural right to happiness and the way Jefferson and his countrymen saw it. To Locke and other European thinkers, a state of happiness, loosely defined as enjoying a free, safe, and comfortable life, was an ideal that could be realized only by the socially well-born and well-to-do. By contrast, American thinkers tended to define the concept of happiness more literally, viewing it as everyone's birthright, regardless of social rank and wealth. Commager explains it this way:

> In the Old World . . . happiness tended to be an elitist concept, something that the privileged few might possibly achieve by cultivating beauty and wisdom and leisure and the social

The Concept of Moral Equality

In this insightful excerpt from his book, From the Declaration of Independence to the Constitution, *former Harvard University scholar Carl J. Friedrich comments on how Jefferson and his American colleagues viewed the concept of equality, on the one hand as an inevitable consequence of natural law, and on the other as a moral rather than literal imperative.*

"To Jefferson and his like-minded contemporaries there was nothing strange in the assertion that the truths of the Declaration were 'self-evident.' The ancient and essentially ethical tradition of natural law, stemming from Cicero and his predecessors, had merged in American thought with the modern Newtonian conception of a universe subject to the 'laws' of physics; and it therefore seemed reasonable that the laws of the moral world, like those of the physical world, would be revealed to him who looked closely at the book of nature. . . . With this concept of the natural order as a starting point, the other 'self-evident' truths of the Declaration fell in line like well-trained guardsmen. For one thing, it is apparent that all men are created equal in the state of nature. This assertion was to be sharply criticized from time to time in succeeding years and to be misunderstood even more often. Critics took it to mean that men are equal in physical and mental endowment, a patent absurdity; and not a few . . . extracted from it the inference that one man's opinion on any subject is as good as the next man's, that the recognition of distinctions between learning and ignorance, between ability and incompetence, is undemocratic. Jefferson and his fellows meant, of course, nothing of the kind. They meant that men were equal in the moral sense and ought to be equal in the political sense. They were drawing on a concept of spiritual equality which was older than Christianity and insisting that the time had come to implement the ideal by erasing legal privileges based on the accident of birth. . . . The principal of equality was already rooted in their experience. On the frontier, which lay only a few short miles from the doors of even urban Americans, artificial distinctions between men tended to dissolve in the common struggle for existence."

The Declaration of Independence asserted that the colonists had a "right" to happiness, regardless of social standing, as exemplified by this scene of family contentment.

> graces: an expensive business, this, and not ordinarily available to the masses of the people. As America had no elite—not, certainly in the Old World sense of the term—happiness here was presumed to be available to all who were white, and it consisted, not in the enjoyment of art and literature, science and philosophy, and social position, but rather in material comfort, freedom, independence, and access to opportunity. Happiness meant milk for the children, and meat on the table, and a well-built house . . . [and] freedom from tyranny of the state, the superstition of the church, [and] the authority of the military.[50]

American patriots not only shared this unique, practical vision of human happiness, they were also ready to do whatever was necessary to ensure its maintenance. When they decided that British policies represented an intolerable threat to their natural rights, including that to personal happiness, Jefferson, Franklin, Adams, and the others took concrete action. They were both justified and obligated, Jefferson stated in the Declaration, "to throw off" despotic government and "to provide new guards for their future security."[51] Their singular achievement, then, was that they selected the best ideas that European intellectuals had to offer and applied them to the political and social realities of America. They turned thought into action and ideals into reality, and in so doing created a momentous turning point in "the course of human events." The Declaration of Independence, with all of its moving references to humane and edifying Enlightenment principles, was in a sense the trumpet blast that signaled that turning point.

Chapter 4 Congress Debates, Revises, and Signs the Declaration

After making minimal changes in Jefferson's rough draft of the Declaration, the drafting committee presented the fair copy of the document to the Congress on June 28, 1776. The delegates temporarily tabled the matter, however. Foremost on their immediate agenda was the then much more pressing business of debating and voting on Lee's resolution for independence, scheduled to begin on July 1. That day the delegates registered their first vote and nine were in the affirmative, the others abstaining because of disagreement within their delegations or lack of authority from their legislatures. More debate, most of it informal, took place late that day and in the following morning. Then came the historic final votes. At first, all of the states except New York were for independence, not because that state's delegates were against the resolution, but because they were still waiting for the go-ahead from their legislature. To everyone's relief, that approval arrived only a few hours later, after which New York voted "yes," making the action unanimous.

In John Trumbull's famous painting, the drafting committee presents the Declaration to Congress. Congressional president John Hancock reportedly remarked, "We must all be unanimous. . . . We must all hang together."

Thus, contrary to popular belief, July 2, 1776, is the actual day that the United States was born. The patriots saw the next order of business, the Declaration of Independence, as important, but more as a formal afterthought; after all, they had no idea at the time that the document would become revered or that the date of its approval would come to be celebrated as the nation's independence day. The historic significance the founders at first attached to the date of July 2 is well illustrated in the correspondence John Adams sent to his wife the next day:

> Yesterday the greatest question was decided which ever was debated in America, and a greater, perhaps, never was nor will be decided among men. A resolution was passed without one dissenting colony, "that these United Colonies are, and of right ought to be, free and independent States, and as such they have, and of right ought to have, full power to make war, conclude peace, establish commerce, and to do all other acts and things which other States may rightfully do." You will see in a few days a Declaration setting forth the causes which have impelled us to this mighty revolution, and the reasons which will justify it in the sight of God and man. . . . The second day of July, 1776, will be the most memorable epocha [event beginning a new era] in the history of America. I am apt to believe that it will be celebrated by succeeding generations as the great anniversary festival. It ought to be commemorated as the day of deliverance, by solemn acts of devotion to God Almighty. It ought to be solemnized with pomp and parade, with shows, games, sports, guns, bells, bonfires and illuminations [fireworks], from one end of this continent to the other, from this time forward, forevermore.[52]

As it happened, of course, the founders' observance of July 2 was in time eclipsed by events they could not foresee and July 4 came to be celebrated as "the great anniversary festival." This is in large part a testimonial to the moving and powerful language and sentiments of the Declaration, which made it irresistibly appealing to succeeding generations.

The Revision Process Begins

Once they had passed Lee's resolution approving the separation of the colonies from the mother country on July 2, the delegates wasted no time in considering the rough draft of the Declaration. Debate on the wording of the Declaration began that day and the revision process continued for almost three solid days, during which Congress made a number of changes, including the deletion of about one-quarter of the text. Some of these changes were relatively minor. For instance, Jefferson had written in his rough draft, "and such is now the necessity which constrains them [the colonies] to expunge their former systems of governments." Congress substituted the word "alter" for "expunge." Similarly, in introducing his list of grievances against the king, Jefferson had stated, "The history of the present king of Great Britain is a history of unremitting injuries and usurpations. . . ." Here, the delegates substituted the word "repeated" for "unremitting."[53]

Other minor changes consisted of the deletion of phrases and partial sentences for the purpose of simplifying and clarifying the text. For example, the rest of the sentence following the phrase "repeated injuries and usurpations" originally read "among which appears no solitary fact to contradict the uniform tenor of the rest, but all have in direct object the establishment of an absolute tyranny over these states." Probably seeing this wording as too complex and scholarly, Congress struck the first seventeen words, replacing them with "all having." This rendered a complete sentence that is shorter, clearer, and more to the point: "The history of the present king of Great Britain is a history of repeated injuries and usurpations, all having in direct object the establishment of an absolute tyranny over these states."[54]

Still another kind of minor revision took the form of additions of new words and phrases, usually for clarification or added emphasis. Among the list of alleged abuses in the rough draft was the king's "giving assent" to acts "for depriving us of the benefits of trial by jury." Here, the delegates apparently felt that the existing phrase might be interpreted to mean that the British had denied the colonists their right to trial by jury in all cases. In fact, infringement of that right had not occurred on a consistent basis in every city and colony; so Congress added the words "in many cases." The result was the more accurate accusation, "for depriving us in many cases of the benefits of trial by jury."

Congress retained the heart of Jefferson's phrase about the "absolute tyranny" of George III (pictured).

While this addition was intended to tone down the original statement, another addition sought to do the opposite, namely to make a statement more forceful. Jefferson had accused the king of "transporting large armies . . . to complete the works of death, desolation and tyranny already begun with circumstances of cruelty and perfidy [treachery] unworthy the head of a civilized nation." The delegates felt that this sentence did not emphasize strongly enough their outrage at such warlike acts. So they inserted nine new words, producing this more provocative version: "to complete the works of death, desolation and tyranny already begun with circumstances of cruelty and perfidy scarcely paralleled in the most barbarous ages, and totally unworthy the head of a civilized nation."[55]

More Substantial Changes

A few of the changes Congress made in Jefferson's rough draft were much more substantial, consisting of the deletion of entire paragraphs. Mostly, these contained strong criticisms or denunciations, some aimed specifically at Parliament and others more generally at the British people. For example, in his rough draft Jefferson reminded his readers and listeners about the circumstances under which British settlers had immigrated to America. Though the colonists had, over the years, remained friendly with Britain and recognized the sovereignty of the British king, he argued, they had set up their own local legislatures; so Parliament's powers over them were limited. "Submission to their parliament was no part of our constitution," he wrote.[56]

Jefferson also complained that those British leaders who advocated keeping America under Parliament's thumb, men he called "the disturbers of our harmony," had continually been reelected. And this had resulted in the enactment of numerous British laws (such as the Intolerable Acts), placing unfair restrictions on the colonies. Even worse, these anti-American leaders had recently sent "not only soldiers of our common blood, but Scotch and foreign mercenaries to invade and destroy us." Considering these facts, Jefferson reasoned in the rough draft, it was necessary for the Americans to "renounce forever these unfeeling brethren," and "to forget our former love for them." Jefferson then added an almost wistful touch of regret, reminding the British of what they had lost: "We might have been a free and great people together." But since sharing the concept of freedom was "below their [i.e., British] dignity," the Americans would gladly tread "the road to happiness" on their own.[57]

Many members of Congress felt uneasy about these forceful statements. In particular, they were worried that these passages might offend and alienate those British citizens and leaders (some of whom served in Parliament) who were sympathetic to the American cause. According to this view, it would be safer and wiser to omit such passages and to keep the thrust of the document's attack focused on the king, who was in a sense more of a symbol than a person. As Jefferson later remembered it:

The pusillanimous [timid] idea that we had friends in England worth keeping terms with, still haunted the minds of many. For this reason, those passages which conveyed censures [criticisms] on the people of England were struck out, lest they should give them offense.[58]

By far the most controversial of Congress's revisions of the Declaration, both at the time and historically, was the deletion of a lengthy passage denouncing the slave trade. One of the great contradictions of Jefferson's life was that he was a slave owner who hated slavery. Intellectually speaking, he considered the institution to be morally wrong; practically speaking, however, he saw that institution as too entrenched, both socially and economically, to be removed without a major and perhaps violent reordering of society. Given the ugly fact of slavery's existence in the colonies, he believed, American leaders should, in founding their new nation, at least take some kind of public moral stand.

Jefferson had already taken such a stand, in the form of a brief statement in the list of grievances he had composed for the preamble to Virginia's constitution. The king had, he charged, "through the inhuman use of his negative . . . refused us permission to exclude [slavery] by law."[59] This suggested that the colonists had always wanted to terminate the slave trade but had been stopped from doing so by British law; so that, in effect, it was the king's and Parliament's fault that slavery had become entrenched, perhaps permanently, in the colonies. This charge was not accurate, since most of the southern colonies had always been and still were eager participants in the slave trade, which constituted one of the primary bases of their economies. But as biographer Ellis points out, blaming the king for the trade "absolved American slaveowners . . . from any responsibility or complicity in the establishment of an institution that was clearly at odds with the values on which the newly independent America was based."[60]

An Assault on the Slave Trade

In writing the rough draft for the Declaration, Jefferson wanted to make this moral stand against the slave trade as strong as possible. So he greatly expanded the small clause he had inserted in the Virginia document. The new version read:

He [the king] has waged cruel war against human nature itself, violating its most sacred rights of life and liberty in the persons of a distant people who never offended him [i.e., black Africans], captivating and carrying them into slavery in another hemisphere, or to incur miserable death in their transportation thither [from there to here]. This piratical warfare, the opprobrium [disgraceful conduct] of infidel powers, is the warfare of the Christian king of Great Britain, determined to keep open a market where men should be bought and sold, he has prostituted his negative for suppressing every legislative attempt to prohibit or to restrain this execrable [repulsive] commerce: and that this assemblage of horrors might want no fact of distinguished die [i.e., if that weren't bad enough], he is now exciting those very people [the slaves] to rise in arms against us, and to purchase that liberty of which he has deprived them, by murdering the people upon whom he also obtruded [forced] them; thus paying off former crimes committed against the liberties of one people, with the crimes which he urges them to commit against the lives of another.[61]

Confronted with this remarkable assault on the slave trade, delegates from several southern states, especially South Carolina and Georgia, were aghast. They strongly opposed any interruption of the trade and were not about to allow such liberal rhetoric to appear in

Revolutionary Sentiments Against Slavery

That Jefferson was not the only American of his era who saw slavery as morally wrong is well illustrated by this excerpt from an antislavery petition presented to the Massachusetts legislature in 1777.

"Your petitioners apprehend that they [black people] have in common with all other men a natural and unalienable right to that freedom which the Great Parent of the Universe [i.e., God] has bestowed equally on all mankind and which they have never forfeited by any compact or agreement whatever—but that were unjustly dragged by the hand of cruel power from their dearest friends and some of them even torn from the embraces of their tender parents—from a populous, pleasant and plentiful country and in violation of [the] laws of nature and of nations . . . brought here . . . to be sold like beasts of burden. . . . Your petitioners have long and patiently waited . . . but with grief [they] reflect that . . . it has never been considered that every principle from which America has acted in the course of [its] unhappy difficulties with Great Britain pleads stronger than a thousand arguments in favor of your petitioners . . . who humbly beseech your honors to . . . [pass an act that would restore blacks] to the enjoyments of that [freedom] which is the natural right of all men."

an important American public document. John Adams, who took Jefferson's side in the matter, later recalled:

> I was delighted with its [the Declaration's] high tone and the flights of oratory with which it abounded, especially that concerning Negro slavery, which, though I knew his Southern brethren would never suffer to pass in Congress, I certainly would never oppose. . . . But they [the delegates] obliterated some of the best of it [the rough draft]. . . . I have long wondered that the original draft had not been published. I suppose the reason is the vehement philippic [forceful attack] against Negro slavery.[62]

Jefferson himself later contended that some northern delegates also favored deleting the slavery clause, since not a few northern ships were involved in the lucrative trade in human cargo:

> Our northern brethren also, I believe, felt a little tender under those censures [criticisms in the clause]; for though their people had very few slaves themselves, yet they had been pretty considerable carriers of them to others.[63]

Surviving the Congressional Gauntlet

While the delegates argued about and deleted the slavery clause, Jefferson sat quietly in his seat, preferring not to take part. "I thought it my duty," he later wrote, "to be, on that occasion, a passive auditor of the opinions of others, more impartial judges than I could be, of its merits and demerits."[64] In fact, he remained passive during the entire three days of debate and revision, less because he thought his colleagues impartial and more because he was so upset about the changes they were making in his original draft. On another later occasion he called these changes "mutilations." Indeed, he was so convinced that Congress had diluted the purity of his vision that in compiling his autobiography many years later, he included the Declaration's first draft, word for word, to make sure that posterity would know his original intentions. He instructed his readers with these words:

> I will state the form of the Declaration as originally reported. The parts struck out by Congress shall be distinguished by a black line drawn under them; and those inserted by them [the delegates] shall be placed in the margin, or in a concurrent column.[65]

Yet not all of the delegates were so inclined to change the fair copy of the document. According to Jefferson's later recollection, John

Adams, one of the leaders of the debate, strenuously, if vainly, attempted to preserve its original integrity: "This . . . I will say about Mr. Adams, that he supported the Declaration with zeal and ability, fighting fearlessly for every word of it."[66] Adams's efforts were not enough to console Jefferson, however, who squirmed in his seat, reacting with anxious or sullen expressions to each revision and deletion. Seeing his plight, Benjamin Franklin sat at his side and did his best to cheer him up. "During the debate," Jefferson recalled in a later letter to another American founder, James Madison,

John Adams, a fiery orator, vigorously fought to keep Jefferson's original wording.

> I was sitting by Dr. Franklin, and he observed that I was writhing a little under the acrimonious [bitter] criticisms of some of its parts; and it was on that occasion, that by way of comfort, he told me the story of John Thompson, the hatter [hatmaker] and his new sign.[67]

According to Jefferson's account in his later biographical sketch of Franklin, the older man told him:

> I have made it a rule, whenever [it is] in my power, to avoid becoming the draftsman of papers to be reviewed by a public body. I took my lesson from an incident which I will relate to you. When I was a journeyman printer, one of my companions, an apprentice hatter, having served out his time, was about to open shop for himself. His first concern was to have a handsome sign-board, with a proper inscription. He composed it in these words, "John Thompson, *Hatter, makes* and *sells hats* for ready money," with a figure of a hat subjoined [attached]; but he thought he would submit it to his friends for their amendments. The first he showed it to thought the word "*Hatter*" tautologous [needlessly repetitive], because [it was] followed by the words "makes hats," which showed he was a hatter. It was struck out. The next [of the hatter's friends] observed that the word "*makes*" might as well be omitted, because his customers would not care who made the hats. If [the hats were] good and to their mind, they would buy [them], by whomsoever [they were] made. He struck it out. A third

[friend] said he thought the words *"for ready money"* [i.e., cash] were useless, as it was not the custom of the place to sell on credit. Everyone who purchased [a hat] expected to pay [cash]. [These words] were parted with, and the inscription now stood, "John Thompson sells hats." *"Sells hats!"* says his next friend. Why nobody will expect you to give them away, [so] what then is the use of that word? It was stricken out, and *"hats"* followed it, the rather [since] there was one painted on the board. So the inscription was reduced ultimately to "John Thompson" with the figure of a hat subjoined.[68]

Franklin's humorous anecdote apparently put Congress's ongoing edit of the Declaration in perspective to some degree and helped to soothe Jefferson during the remainder of his ordeal. In retrospect, Jefferson need not have fretted about the revisions and how history would view them. Later historians have been almost unanimous in the opinion that these changes helped rather than hurt the document, making it more concise, understandable, and powerful. Historian Dumas Malone, for example, thinks the deletion of the controversial slavery clause was no loss. The inaccurate charge that the British Crown was solely responsible for the slave trade, he says, "was really

Jefferson reads the Declaration's rough draft to Franklin, who later consoled the anxious younger man during the revision process.

out of character with the rest of the document. It was one of those rare Jeffersonian passages which are consciously rhetorical [concerned with speech making] and betray a striving for effect [rather than substance]."[69] Jefferson biographer Merrill Peterson agrees, adding:

> Jefferson seemed to feel that the Declaration, after passing through the gauntlet of Congress, emerged a weaker document. In fact, it gained in every respect. Congress corrected him precisely where he had allowed himself to go astray: in entering technical legal points, in making loose, circuitous [roundabout or rambling], or wordy statements, and in using declamatory [rhetorical] language. Cleared of these aberrations, the intrinsic [inherent] merits of the work stood in bolder relief than when it passed from Jefferson's hands.[70]

Ratifying and Signing the Document

Congress finished its revision of the Declaration of Independence late in the day on July 4, 1776. The dramatic historical scene so often depicted in later years, namely of all the delegates ratifying and signing the document at that moment, is a popular fiction. The actual ratification and signing process was much more complex and drawn out. Because the exact circumstances became confused or forgotten over the years, in Henry Commager's words, "an impenetrable cloud conceals the actual history of the signing."[71]

Historians have, however, managed to piece together a plausible reconstruction of that history. First, on July 4, with debate and revision complete, twelve of the thirteen states agreed to adopt the Declaration as a written expression of Lee's resolution on independence. The delegates from New York did not vote and it was not until July 15, when that state's legislature approved the document, that its acceptance became unanimous. Meanwhile, sometime between July 5 and 7, several copies of the document were printed and sent via couriers to the various state assemblies and leading military officers. On July 8, according to a brief mention in one of John Adams's letters, the Declaration's first public reading took place in the yard of Philadelphia's state house. The large crowd that had gathered there cheered loudly, after which the local militia paraded to the town common and bells rang through most of the night, a scene reenacted, with minor variations, all across America in the weeks that followed.

These initial few printed copies of the Declaration bore no signatures. Apparently, no one signed the document on July 4, except for John Hancock, the president of the Congress (and possibly Charles Thomson, the congressional secretary), mainly to authenticate that this was the version agreed on.[72] It was not until July 19 that Congress or-

Agreeing to Their Own Death Warrants?

In this portion of a letter written to John Adams in August 1776, shortly after the official signing of the Declaration, Pennsylvania delegate Benjamin Rush remembers an amusing moment during the otherwise solemn day (July 2) on which Congress voted for independence.

"The 4th of July has been celebrated in Philadelphia in the manner I expected. The military men, and particularly one of them, ran away with all the glory of the day. Scarcely a word was said of the solitude and labors and fears and sorrows and sleepless nights of the men who projected, proposed, defended, and subscribed the Declaration of Independence. Do you recollect your memorable speech upon the day on which the vote [on independence] was taken? Do you recollect the pensive and awful silence which pervaded the house when we were called up, one after another, to the table of the President of Congress to subscribe [agree to] what was believed by many at the time to be our own death warrants? The silence and the gloom of the morning was interrupted, I well recollect, only for a moment by Colonel [Benjamin] Harrison of Virginia, who said to Mr. [Elbridge] Gerry [of Massachusetts] . . . 'I shall have a great advantage over you, Mr. Gerry, when we are all hung for what we are doing. From the size and weight of my body I shall die in a few minutes, but from the lightness of your body you will dance in the air an hour or two before you are dead.'"

dered the Declaration to be transferred to parchment and signed by the members. That same day, Congress also decided that the document should bear the title "The Unanimous Declaration of the 13 United States of America." The formal signing ceremony took place on August 2, at which time Jefferson, the principal author, probably affixed his signature to the work. However, some of the members were unable to attend the ceremony. So they signed the document in the following few days and weeks. In all, fifty-six members of Congress signed it, although their signatures were not made public until January 1777.

This turned out to be only the beginning of the Declaration's history, one that no one at the time foresaw. At first, people viewed the document simply as a formal affirmation of an accomplished fact, namely American independence from Britain. In time, however, it would become the chief symbol and statement of the American creed. And the democratic principles it espoused would slowly but surely transform the new nation, and eventually the world, beyond all recognition.

The Widespread Influence of the Declaration's Ideals

The parchment copy of the Declaration of Independence signed by the members of Congress beginning on August 2, 1776, has fortunately survived. This is remarkable considering how the document, viewed as one of the most important and precious of all American artifacts, has suffered from the ravages of aging and near destruction. In the first 176 years of its existence, the Declaration had no permanent home. In the late 1700s and on into the 1800s, it moved frequently from place to place, as local officials exhibited it in at least ten cities in five states. During these years, it narrowly escaped destruction by fire on two occasions. In addition, during both the Revolutionary War and War of 1812, the British almost captured it, an event that would have been a serious blow to American national pride.

By 1894, the toll that time had taken on the document had become a matter of concern; too much exposure to light had dimmed its ink and some of the historic signatures had been damaged by repeated rolling and unrolling of the parchment. So that year, hoping to slow such deterioration, officials placed the Declaration in a safe in the library of the U.S. Department of State. In 1921, they moved it once more, this time to the Library of Congress. Finally, in 1952, the document found a permanent resting place in a display case in the exhibition hall of the National Archives in Washington, D.C. There, tens of thousands of people, both Americans and foreigners, file by each year to see firsthand this renowned and revered relic that was once handled by the likes of Thomas Jefferson, John Adams, and Benjamin Franklin.

As the original document wandered the United States in its initial century or so, the influence of the democratic principles it espoused traveled a good deal farther. In creating the world's first modern large-scale democracy and then going on to defeat Britain, at the time the strongest nation on earth, the American founders set an inspiring example for others who dreamed of freedom and independence. But could this brave new government of and by the people survive in a world still dominated by powerful monarchies? At first, many foreign leaders thought it could not. Indeed, the British were still confident that they could regain their former American colonies when the two nations clashed in the War of 1812.

However, the United States proved its doubters wrong by surviving that war and other crises in decade after decade. It showed a world long accustomed to kings and dictators that a government ruled by the people could, after all, prevail as a viable working system. And all the while, as the United States grew steadily larger and militarily stronger, its political institutions kept pace. Over time they became increasingly more democratic, thereby affording more and more minorities and other groups a chance to share in the American dream. The result is that many millions of people in the past two centuries have been able to exercise the right to happiness that Jefferson cited as a primary human birthright in the Declaration.

Waking from the Sleep of Despotism

The first and most immediate influence exerted by the Declaration's liberal principles was over France, which had helped the United States in its war of independence. At the time of this conflict, France was fast approaching the brink of serious economic and social disaster. The French people had been for some time growing increasingly restless and unhappy, partly because the country's social structure was rigid, in many ways class-oriented and unjust, and increasingly outmoded. Making matters worse, their last king, Louis XV (who had died in 1774), had wasted large sums of money on costly wars and personal luxuries; while his successor, Louis XVI, was a well-meaning but indecisive and ineffectual ruler under whom the national treasury continued to shrink. The most lasting achievement of these rulers was to make a majority of the French people resentful and suspicious of the monarchy.

Thus, France was ripe for revolution. And it is hardly surprising that many French citizens were fascinated with and inspired by the American Revolution, which they saw as having been fought to achieve the democratic principles stated in its stirring Declaration of Independence. In his autobiography, Jefferson later recalled:

> Celebrated writers of France and England [such as Montesquieu and Locke] had already sketched good principles on the subject of government; yet the American Revolution seems first to have awakened the thinking part of the French nation in general, from the sleep of despotism in which they were sunk. The [French] officers too, who had been to America, were mostly young men, less shackled by habit and prejudice, and more ready to assent to the suggestions of common sense, and feeling of common rights, than others. They came back with new ideas and impressions. The press, notwithstanding its shackles, began to disseminate them; conversation assumed new freedoms; politics became the theme of all societies

King Louis XVI of France finds himself threatened by an angry mob in June 1792.

> [social circles], male and female, and a very extensive and zealous party was formed, which acquired the appellation of the Patriotic party, who, sensible of the abusive government under which they had lived, sighed for occasions of reforming it.[73]

Many such French reformers saw America's new democracy as a model to imitate. The popular writer Abbé Gentil suggested that the democratic spirit unleashed in the United States would one day spread across the world; while another writer, Abbé Robin, who penned several works about America and its people, was enthusiastic about the apparent lack of class distinctions in that land. When an American army makes camp, he reported, officers, soldiers, American men and women, all join and dance together. . . . These people are still in the happy time when distinctions of birth and rank are ignored and can see, with the same eye, the common soldier and the officer.[74]

The French Declaration of Rights

Similarly, during the first stages of the French Revolution, in 1789, French patriots recognized the need to write a document that stated basic human rights in the same manner as the American Declaration. The first to submit a draft for a French declaration was the marquis de Lafayette (1757–1834), an army officer who had fought alongside and become a close friend of George Washington in the American Revolution. In the summer of 1789, Lafayette composed a number of drafts and asked Jefferson, then serving in Paris as U.S. ambassador to France, to look them over. Jefferson did so, making several additions based on his personal experiences in drafting American political documents.

Unfortunately for Lafayette, his version of the declaration received little attention in the French National Assembly, the new legislature that claimed to be France's rightful government. Other members of the assembly produced their own version and issued it on August 27 of that year under the title of The Declaration of the Rights of Man and the Citizen. This famous document was more radical than the American Declaration and drew its ideas and language more directly from the ideas of Enlightenment writers like Locke than from Jefferson and the American experience. Also, the French declaration's format—a list of basic rights—bore a much closer resemblance to the American Bill of Rights (ratified in 1791) than to the American Declaration.

Yet the American revolutionary experience, for which Jefferson's Declaration had provided a strong rationale, had set an example for French revolutionaries. While the American fight for independence did not cause or incite the French Revolution, it showed the French that such a fight could actually be waged and won by people with a just cause. The marquis de Condorcet, an Enlightenment philosopher and member of the French Assembly, put it this way:

> It is not enough that human rights should be written in the books of philosophers and in the hearts of virtuous men; it is necessary that ignorant or weak men should read them in the example of a great people. America has given us this example. The act which declares its independence is a simple and sublime exposition of those rights so sacred and so long forgotten.[75]

Inspiring a Spirit of Resistance

Despite the sincerity of French patriots, their elimination of the French monarchy, and the establishment of representative government in France, the French Revolution did not produce a workable, stable democracy, as had happened in America. France continued to seethe in turmoil throughout the 1790s, as various experimental governments rose and fell. The end result in the short run was military

The French Declaration of the Rights of Man and the Citizen

Passed by the French National Assembly on August 27, 1789, the French declaration, excerpted here, attempted to define democratic principles similar to those that Jefferson had spelled out in the American Declaration.

"The representatives of the people of France, formed into a National Assembly, considering that ignorance, neglect, or contempt of human rights, are the sole causes of public misfortunes and corruptions of government, have resolved to set forth in a solemn declaration these natural . . . and inalienable rights. . . .

1. Men are born and always continue, free and equal in respect of their rights. Civil distinctions, therefore, can be founded only on public utility.
2. The end [goal] of all political associations is the preservation of the natural . . . rights of man; and these rights are Liberty, Property, Security, and Resistance of Oppression. . . .
6. The law is the expression of the will of the community. All citizens have a right to concur, either personally or by their representatives, in its formation.
7. No man should be accused, arrested, or held in confinement, except in cases determined by the law, and according to the forms which it has prescribed. . . .
10. No man ought to be molested on account of his opinions, not even on account of his religious opinions, provided his avowal of them does not disturb the public order established by the law. . . .
14. Every citizen has a right, either by himself or his representative, to a free voice in determining the necessity of public contributions [taxes], the appropriations [raising] of them, and their amount. . . .
17. The right to property being inviolable [safe from violation] and sacred, no one ought to be deprived of it."

dictatorship (under Napoleon Bonaparte) and it took France several more decades to achieve real democracy.

In the meantime, the democratic principles of the French Revolution, which had been partly inspired by those of the American version, directly inspired revolutionary activity in many other lands. Both the American and French declarations had spelled out the right of the people to oppose oppressive government. Both had also proclaimed human rights, promising equality for all; although the French attempt to institute such rights had been more radical, violent, and, at least in Europe, more influential than the American one. From the French Revolution onwards, comments historian J. L. Talmon, "any injury to what came to be thought of as the dignity of man, began to appear as intolerable, and justifying resistance."[76]

The spirit of such resistance grew into a revolutionary fervor that exploded across Europe in 1848. That year the French created their Second Republic, which reestablished their revolutionary ideals and at the same time touched off uprisings all over the continent. The Austrian people rose up and forced their emperor off his throne, and his successor had to adopt fairer, more liberal political policies. In Hungary, the people demanded and won a new constitution that recognized several basic human rights. And demands for political reform echoed through Germany, Italy, and other nations. At the time, none of these countries completely discarded their old systems and became democracies. Yet the ideas of liberty, social equality, and popular government had taken firm root in European soil. In time, after numerous wars, revolutions, and political struggles, democratic systems would become the rule there.

In some other parts of the world, the influence of the American Revolution and Jefferson's Declaration and its ideals was more direct. In 1810, for instance, local patriots in Venezuela, in South America, began a revolution to gain independence from their mother country, Spain. One of the leaders of the revolution, Francisco de Miranda (1750–1816), who had fought in both the American and French Revolutions, was particularly inspired by the American Declaration and its rationales for independence and freedom.[77] The American democratic system also profoundly influenced the establishment of representative governments in Argentina (in South America, 1816), Liberia (in western Africa, 1847), the Philippines (in the South Pacific, 1946), and several Central American countries. And in 1945, when Vietnam's revolutionary leader, Ho Chi Minh, proclaimed his land's independence, he modeled his declaration on the one Jefferson had penned in 1776.

The American Encounter

The democratic system inaugurated by the American Declaration of Independence was most influential in the twentieth century. Dozens of democracies were established around the world in that century, reaching an unprecedented total of seventy-five in 1992; and in the majority of cases, the United States sponsored, aided, and/or inspired the initiation of these regimes. This turn of events occurred partly because the United States became a military superpower in these years and used its authority and prestige to spread democracy around the globe; however, an even more powerful factor was the phenomenal success of the nation's market economy and its resultant wealth and high living standards. Having been achieved largely through the spirit of free private enterprise, or capitalism, this economic success was among the fortunate fruits of a long-lived and open democratic system. And this fact was not lost on numerous nations seeking the same sort of success. In the words of political scholars James Hoge and Fareed Zakaria:

> Life at the end of the twentieth century is dominated by the idea and the reality of America's distinctive creed, liberal democratic capitalism. Nations and peoples of every culture are adapting their old world to these new ideas, and their countries are being revolutionized, slowly but surely, by it. Some of this transformation is the result of broad structural shifts like industrialization and modernization, but much of it is the result of one nation's efforts to stand for and fight for certain political and economic ideals. The American encounter has changed the world.[78]

Indeed, part of that change has been the near global acceptance of American values (or more properly, Enlightenment values absorbed and advocated by the United States). "In every century," former U.S. secretary of state Henry Kissinger once remarked, "there seems to emerge a country with the power, the will and the intellectual and moral impetus to shape the entire international system in accordance with its own values."[79] Thus, Spain largely shaped the course of world events in the sixteenth century, France in the seventeenth, and Britain in the nineteenth; the twentieth, however, was unarguably the American century. Because of its enormous economic success and the desire of others to imitate or share in it, the United States was able to export many of the democratic ideas mentioned in the Declaration of Independence.

One significant way the United States did this was to make sure that such ideas were incorporated into important international agreements. The most influential and famous such accord is the char-

The United Nations Universal Declaration of Human Rights

Following are a few of the articles listed in the declaration adopted by the United Nations on December 6, 1948. Although the organization lacks the authority to enforce these rights in individual countries, it continues to work in nonviolent ways to persuade member nations to treat their citizens with dignity and respect.

"1. All human beings are born free and equal in dignity and rights. They are endowed with reason and conscience and should act towards one another in a spirit of brotherhood.

2. Everyone is entitled to all the rights and freedoms set forth in this Declaration, without distinction of any kind, such as race, color, sex, language, religion, political or other opinion, national or social origin, property, birth, or other status. . . .

3. Everyone has the right to life, liberty, and security of person.

4. No one shall be held in slavery or servitude; slavery and the slave trade shall be prohibited in all their forms. . . .

6. Everyone has the right to recognition everywhere as a person before the law. . . .

9. No one shall be subjected to arbitrary arrest, detention, or exile. . . .

13. Everyone has the right to freedom of movement and residence within the borders of each state. Everyone has the right to leave any country, including his own, and to return to his country. . . .

17. Everyone has the right to own property alone as well as in association with others. No one shall be arbitrarily deprived of his property. . . .

19. Everyone has the right to freedom of opinion and expression. . . .

21. Everyone has the right to take part in the Government of his country, directly or through freely chosen representatives.

27. Everyone has the right to freely participate in the cultural life of the community, to enjoy the arts, and to share in scientific advancement and its benefits."

ter of the United Nations, containing the Declaration of Human Rights, adopted on December 6, 1948. Reproducing the sentiments and sometimes even the language of the American Declaration and Bill of Rights (as well as the French Declaration and English Bill of Rights), the UN Declaration proclaims in part:

> All human beings are born free and equal in dignity and rights. They are endowed with reason and conscience and

should act towards one another in a spirit of brotherhood. . . . Everyone has the right to life, liberty, and security of person. . . . Everyone has the right to recognition everywhere as a person before the law. . . . Everyone has the right to own property alone as well as in association with others. . . . Everyone has the right to freedom of opinion and expression. . . . Everyone has the right to take part in the Government of his country, directly or through freely chosen representatives.[80]

The Revolution's Transforming Hand

Although the application of American democratic values has been widespread around the world, nowhere have these values had more direct or profound influence than in the United States itself. Indeed, says noted historian Ralph B. Perry, "The history of American democracy is a gradual realization, too slow for some and too rapid for others, of the implications of the Declaration of Independence."[81] Biographer Joseph Ellis expresses the same view, identifying some of the groups affected by this still ongoing social revolution:

> The entire history of liberal reform in America can be written as a process of discovery, within Jefferson's words, of a spiritually sanctioned mandate for ending slavery, providing the rights of citizenship to blacks and women, justifying welfare programs for the poor and expanding individual freedoms.[82]

The American Revolution was certainly not a social revolution at the time. Jefferson, Adams, Washington, and the other American leaders, all of them well-to-do white males, essentially traded domination by foreign aristocrats for a similar kind of rule by members of the American social elite. Their revolution left society itself more or less unchanged: People with no property still had little or no political voice, women remained second-class citizens who could not vote, and blacks continued to suffer the cruelties of slavery. Despite the statement about equality and other liberal rhetoric of the Declaration, American society was still decidedly *un*equal. On the surface, therefore, the American founders' revolution was mainly a political one.

What Jefferson and his fellows did not realize at the time was that in a very real sense their revolution did not end in 1783 with their triumphant defeat of the mother country. That event marked merely the end of the fight for political independence. In reality, the revolution had only just begun, for the founders had created a new and daring kind of government, one built firmly on the *ideas* of equality and democratic opportunity for all. And although these concepts existed mainly on paper at first, over time increasing numbers of Americans of all walks of life came to see them as their birthright and demanded to benefit from them. In his classic statement of social revolution, the renowned American historian J. Franklin Jameson wrote:

> The stream of revolution, once started, could not be confined within narrow banks, but spread abroad upon the land. Many economic desires, many social aspirations were set free by the political struggle, many aspects of colonial society profoundly altered by the forces thus let loose. The relations of social classes to one another, the institution of slavery, the system of land-holding, the course of business, the forms and spirit of the intellectual and religious life, all felt the transforming hand of revolution, all emerged from under it in shapes advanced many degrees nearer to those we know.[83]

The Most Modern People in the World

Indeed, the revolution's "transforming hand," still guided by the principles set forth in Jefferson's Declaration, set in motion the ideological and social forces that reshaped American society. In each succeeding generation, group after group became in a sense new revolutionaries, who took Adams, Jefferson, and the others at their word, demanded their rights, and finally, often after long and difficult struggles, began to enjoy these rights. Antislavery societies first formed in America during the revolutionary period. These gained strength and, combined with other changing social and economic factors, led inevitably to the Civil War and abolition of slavery. Women increasingly lobbied for and gained their rights, including the right to vote. Meanwhile, nearly all of the class and economic barriers that had existed in the late 1700s were swept away in the continuing American revolution. "In 1760," scholar Gordon S. Wood remarks,

> America was only a collection of disparate colonies huddled along a narrow strip of the Atlantic coast—economically underdeveloped outposts existing on the very edges of the civilized world. The less than two million monarchical subjects who lived in these colonies still took for granted that society was and ought to be a hierarchy [ladder] of ranks and degrees of dependency and that most people were bound together by personal ties of one sort or another. Yet scarcely fifty years later these insignificant borderland provinces had become a giant, almost continent-wide republic of nearly ten million egalitarian-minded bustling citizens who not only had thrust themselves into the vanguard [forefront] of history, but had fundamentally altered their society and

> their social relationships. Far from remaining monarchical, hierarchy-ridden subjects on the margin of civilization, Americans had become, almost overnight, the most liberal, the most democratic, the most commercially minded, and the most modern people in the world.[84]

These sweeping social changes continued and in fact accelerated in the twentieth century. In battle after battle, one minority group after another fought for civil rights, justice, and fair treatment under

During the ongoing American rights revolution, American women known as "suffragettes" repeatedly asked their countrymen to "help us to win the vote."

Thousands of picketers demand equal rights for black Americans in the now famous 1963 civil rights march on Washington, D.C.

the democratic constitutional framework created by the founding fathers. Thus, in breaking away from Britain and establishing the most open democracy in history, the American revolutionaries set in motion a mighty social revolution that has continued to the present and shows no signs of letting up. There can be little doubt that this struggle to transform the ideals of the Declaration of Independence into reality will not cease until all groups have achieved true equality. That is the powerful living legacy of the document.

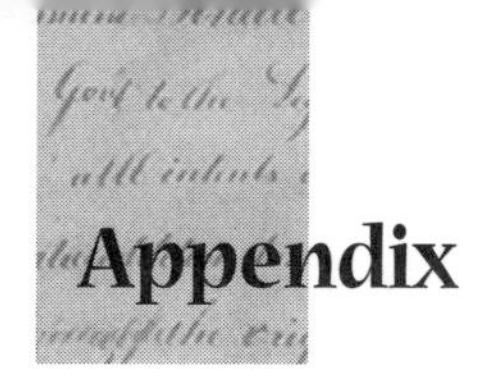

Appendix

Excerpts from Original Documents Pertaining to the Declaration of Independence

Document 1: The Declaration of Independence

This is the final version of the document, accepted by the Continental Congress on July 4, 1776, after two days of debate and revision.

WHEN in the Course of human events, it becomes necessary for one people to dissolve the political bands which have connected them with another, and to assume among the Powers of the earth, the separate and equal Station to which the Laws of Nature and of Nature's God entitle them, a decent respect to the opinions of mankind requires that they should declare the causes which impel them to the separation.—We hold these truths to be self-evident, that all men are created equal, that they are endowed by their Creator with certain unalienable Rights, that among these are Life, Liberty, and the pursuit of Happiness.—That to secure these rights, Governments are instituted among Men, deriving their just powers from the consent of the governed.—That whenever any Form of Government becomes destructive of these ends, it is the Right of the People to alter or to abolish it, and to institute new Government, laying its foundation on such principles and organizing its powers in such form, as to them shall seem most likely to effect their Safety and Happiness. Prudence, indeed, will dictate that Governments long established should not be changed for light and transient causes; and accordingly all experience hath shewn, that mankind are more disposed to suffer, while evils are sufferable, than to right themselves by abolishing the forms to which they are accustomed. But when a long train of abuses and usurpations, pursuing invariably the same Object, evinces a design to reduce them under absolute Despotism, it is their right, it is their duty, to throw off such Government, and to provide new Guards for their future security.—Such has been the patient sufferance of these Colonies; and such is now the necessity which constrains them to alter their former System of Government. The history of the present King of Great Britain is a history of repeated injuries and usurpations, all having in direct object the establishment of an absolute Tyranny over these States. To prove this, let the Facts be submitted to a candid world.—He has refused his Assent to Laws, the most wholesome and necessary for the public good.—He has forbidden his Governors to pass Laws of immediate and pressing importance, unless suspended in their operation till his Assent should be obtained; and when so suspended, he has utterly neglected to attend to them.—He has refused to pass other Laws for the accommodation of large districts of people, unless those people would relinquish the right of Representation in the Legislature, a right inestimable to them and formidable to tyrants only.—He has called together legislative bodies at places unusual, uncomfortable, and distant from the depository of their public Records, for the sole purpose of fatiguing them into compliance with his measures.—He has dissolved Representative Houses repeatedly, for oppressing with manly firmness his invasions on the rights of the people.—He has refused for a long time, after such dissolutions, to cause others to be elected; whereby the Legislative powers, incapable of Annihilation, have returned to the People at large for their exercise; the State remaining in the mean time exposed to all the dangers of invasion from without, and convulsions within.—He has endeavored to prevent the population of these States; for that purpose obstructing Laws for naturalization of Foreigners; refusing to pass others to encourage their migrations hither, and raising the conditions of new Appropriations of Lands.—He has obstructed the Administration of Justice, by refusing his Assent to Laws for establishing Judiciary Powers.—He has made Judges dependent on his Will alone, for the tenure of their offices, and the amount and payment of their salaries.—He has erected a multitude of New Offices, and sent hither swarms of Officers to harass our people, and eat out their substance.—He has kept among us, in times of peace, Standing Armies without the Consent of our Legislatures.—He has affected to render the Military independent of and superior to the Civil power.—He has combined with others to subject us to a jurisdiction foreign to our constitution, and unacknowledged by our laws; giving his Assent to their Acts of pretended Legislation:—For quartering large bodies of armed troops among us:—For protecting them by a mock Trial, from punishment for any Murders which they should commit on the Inhabitants of these States:—For cutting off our Trade with all parts of the World:—For imposing Taxes on us without our Consent:—For depriving us in many cases of the benefits of Trial by Jury:—For transporting us beyond Seas to be tried for pretended offenses:—For abolishing the free System of English Laws in a neighboring—Province, establishing therein an Arbitrary government, and enlarging its Boundaries so as to render it at once an example and fit instrument for introducing the same absolute rule into these Colonies:—For taking away our Charters, abolishing our most valuable Laws, and altering fundamentally the Forms of our Governments:—For suspending our own Legislatures, and declaring themselves invested with power to legislate for us in all cases whatsoever.—He has abdicated Government here, by declaring us out of his Protection and waging war against us.—He has plundered our seas, ravaged our Coasts, burnt our towns, and destroyed the lives of our people.—He is at this time transporting large Armies of foreign Mercenaries to complete the works of death, desolation and tyranny, already begun with circumstances of Cruelty and perfidy scarcely paralleled in the most barbarous ages, and totally unworthy the Head of a civilized nation.—He has constrained our fellow Citizens taken captive on the high Seas to bear Arms against their Country, to become the executioners of their friends and Brethren, or to fall themselves by their Hands.—He has excited domestic insurrections amongst us, and has endeavored to bring on the inhabitants of our frontiers, the merciless Indian Savages, whose rule of warfare is an undistinguished destruction of all ages, sexes and conditions. In every stage of these Oppressions We have Petitioned for Redress in the most humble terms. Our repeated Petitions have been answered only by repeated injury. A Prince, whose character is thus Marked by every act which may define a Tyrant, is unfit to be the ruler of a free people. —Nor have We been wanting in attentions to our British brethren. We have warned them from time to time of attempts by their legislature to extend an unwarrantable jurisdiction over us. We have reminded them of the circumstances of our emigration and settlement here. We have appealed to their native justice and magnanimity, and we have conjured them by the ties of our common kindred to disavow these usurpations, which would inevitably interrupt our connections and correspondence. They too have been deaf to the voice of justice and of consanguinity. We must, therefore, acquiesce in the necessity which denounces our Separation, and hold them, as we hold the rest of mankind, Enemies in War, in Peace Friends.

WE THEREFORE, the Representatives of the UNITED STATES OF AMERICA, in General Congress, Assembled, appealing to the Supreme Judge of the world for the rectitude of our intentions, do, in the Name, and by the authority of the good People of these Colonies, solemnly publish and declare, That these United Colonies are and of Right ought to be FREE AND INDEPENDENT STATES; that they are Absolved from all Allegiance to the British Crown, and that all political connection between them and the State of Great Britain, is and ought to be totally dissolved; and that as Free and Independent States, they have full Power to levy War, conclude Peace, contract Alliances, establish Commerce, and to do all other Acts and Things which Independent States may of right do. And for the support of this Declaration, with a firm reliance on the protection of Divine Providence, We mutually pledge to each other our Lives, our Fortunes, and our sacred Honor.

Document 2: "We Might Have Been a Free and Great People Together"

Following is Congress's complete revision of the sections of the rough draft in which Jefferson had strongly criticized the British people. The deleted passages are both italicized and bracketed and the additions are in upper case.

Nor have we been wanting in attentions to our British brethren. We have warned them from time to time of attempts by their legislature to extend AN UNWARRANTABLE [*a*] jurisdiction over US [*these our states*]. We have reminded them of the circumstances of our emigration and settlement here, [*no one of which could warrant so strange a pretension: that these were effected at the expense of our own blood and treasure, unassisted by the wealth or the strength of Great Britain: that in constituting indeed our several forms of government, we had adopted one common king, thereby laying a foundation for perpetual league and amity with them; but that submission to their parliament was no part of our constitution, nor ever in idea, if history may be credited: and,*] we HAVE appealed to their native justice and magnanimity AND WE HAVE CONJURED THEM BY [*as well as to*] the ties of our common kindred to disavow these usurpations which WOULD INEVITABLY [*were likely to*] interrupt our connection and correspondence. They too have been deaf to the voice of justice and consanguinity. WE MUST THEREFORE [*and when occasions have been given them, by the regular course of their laws, of removing from their councils the disturbers of our harmony, they have, by their free election, re-established them in power. At this very time too, they are permitting their chief magistrate to send over not only soldiers of our common blood, but Scotch and foreign mercenaries to invade and destroy us. These facts have given the last stab to agonizing affection, and manly spirit bids us to renounce forever these unfeeling brethren. We must endeavor to forget our former love for them, and hold them as we would hold the rest of mankind, enemies in war, in peace friends. We might have been a free and great people together; but a communication of grandeur and of freedom, it seems, is below their dignity. Be it so, since they will have it. The road to happiness and to glory is open to us, too. We will tread it apart from them, and*] acquiesce in the necessity which denounces our [*eternal*] separation. AND HOLD THEM AS WE HOLD THE REST OF MANKIND, ENEMIES IN WAR, IN PEACE FRIENDS!

Source Notes

Introduction: The Documentary Symbol of American Union

1. Quoted in Henry S. Commager and Richard B. Morris, eds., *The Spirit of 'Seventy-Six: The Story of the American Revolution as Told by Participants*. 2 vols. New York: Bobbs-Merrill, 1958, vol. 1, pp. 322–23.
2. Dumas Malone, *Jefferson the Virginian*. Boston: Little, Brown, 1948, p. 223.
3. Letter to H. L. Pierce et al., April 6, 1859, quoted in Malone, *Jefferson the Virginian*, p. 226.
4. "The Declaration of Independence," in Lally Weymouth, ed., *Thomas Jefferson: The Man, His World, His Influence*. London: Weidenfeld and Nicolson, 1973, p. 183.
5. Joseph J. Ellis, *American Sphinx: The Character of Thomas Jefferson*. New York: Knopf, 1997, p. 54.
6. Quoted in Commager and Morris, *Spirit of 'Seventy-Six*, vol. 1, p. 321.

Chapter 1: The Origins and Growth of the Spirit of '76

7. In 1607, the London Company, a trading corporation, established the colony of Jamestown, on what is now the coast of Virginia; in 1624, the organization, by now renamed the Virginia Company, lost its charter, which subsequently passed into the hands of the British Crown.
8. Richard Hofstadter et al., *The United States: The History of a Republic*. Englewood Cliffs, NJ: Prentice-Hall, 1957, p. 43.
9. Samuel E. Morison, *The Oxford History of the American People*. New York: Oxford University Press, 1965, p. 180.
10. Quoted in Edmund S. Morgan and Helen M. Morgan, *The Stamp Act Crisis: Prologue to Revolution*. Chapel Hill: University of North Carolina Press, 1953, p. 37.
11. Harry M. Ward, *The American Revolution: Nationhood Achieved, 1763–1788*. New York: St. Martin's Press, 1995, pp. 34–35.
12. Quoted in Richard B. Morris, ed., *The American Revolution, 1763–1783: A Bicentennial Collection*. Columbia: University of South Carolina Press, 1970, p. 80.
13. Quoted in Samuel E. Morison, ed., *Sources and Documents Illustrating the American Revolution, 1764–1788, and the Formation of the Federal Constitution*. Oxford: Clarendon Press, 1953, p. 53.
14. *Massachusetts Gazette*, December 23, 1773, quoted in Morris, *The American Revolution*, p. 124.

15. Quoted in Commager and Morris, *Spirit of 'Seventy-Six*, vol. 1, p. 39. This spontaneous meeting was technically illegal, since Virginia's governor had only hours before dissolved the Virginia legislature after its members had resolved that the Boston Port Act was a "hostile invasion" of the colonies.
16. *Declaration and Resolves of the First Continental Congress*, quoted in Morison, *Sources and Documents*, pp. 119, 122.
17. Thomas Paine, *Common Sense*, in *John Dos Passos Presents the Living Thoughts of Tom Paine*. New York: Fawcett, 1963, pp. 60, 78.

Chapter 2: The Declaration's Composition and Initial Revision

18. Quoted in A. A. Lipscomb and A. E. Bergh, eds., *The Writings of Thomas Jefferson*. 20 vols. Washington, DC: Thomas Jefferson Memorial Association of the United States, 1903, vol. 16, p. 372.
19. Letter to James Warren, May 20, 1776, in Commager and Morris, *Spirit of 'Seventy-Six*, vol. 1, p. 295.
20. Quoted in Adrienne Koch and William Peden, eds., *The Life and Selected Writings of Thomas Jefferson*. New York: Random House, 1944, p. 14.
21. Quoted in Koch and Peden, *Life and Selected Writings of Thomas Jefferson*, pp. 19–20.
22. Ellis, *American Sphinx*, p. 49.
23. Letter to Timothy Pickering, August 6, 1822, in Commager and Morris, *Spirit of 'Seventy-Six*, vol. 1, p. 313.
24. Quoted in Commager and Morris, *Spirit of 'Seventy-Six*, vol. 1, p. 312.
25. Letter to Timothy Pickering, August 6, 1822, in Commager and Morris, *Spirit of 'Seventy-Six*, vol. 1, pp. 313–14.
26. Graff's house was demolished in 1883; the historic desk is now on display at the National Museum in Washington, DC.
27. This and the following quotes from Jefferson's rough draft can be found in Koch and Peden, *Life and Selected Writings of Thomas Jefferson*, pp. 22–28 and also in Carl Becker, *The Declaration of Independence: A Study in the History of Political Ideas*. New York: Harcourt, Brace and Company, 1922, pp. 141–51.
28. Letter to James Madison, August 30, 1823, quoted in Commager and Morris, *Spirit of 'Seventy-Six*, vol. 1, p. 314.
29. Becker, *Declaration of Independence*, pp. 153–56.
30. Merrill D. Peterson, *Thomas Jefferson and the New Nation*. New York: Oxford University Press, 1970, pp. 90–91.

Chapter 3: The Enlightened Ideas that Inspired the Declaration

31. Quoted in Commager and Morris, *Spirit of 'Seventy-Six*, vol. 1, p. 315.

32. Quoted in Commager and Morris, *Spirit of 'Seventy-Six*, vol. 1, p. 315.
33. Carl J. Friedrich and Robert G. McCloskey, eds., *From the Declaration of Independence to the Constitution: The Roots of American Constitutionalism*. Indianapolis: Bobbs-Merrill, 1954, p. xxxix.
34. Peterson, *Thomas Jefferson*, p. 90.
35. Letter to James Madison, August 30, 1823, and "Letter of May 8, 1825, to Henry Lee," in Commager and Morris, *Spirit of 'Seventy-Six*, vol. 1, p. 315.
36. *Preamble to Virginia Constitution*, in Edward Dumbauld, *The Declaration of Independence and What It Means Today*. Norman: University of Oklahoma Press, 1950, pp. 162–63; and *Declaration of Independence*, in Koch and Peden, *Life and Selected Writings of Thomas Jefferson*, pp. 23–25.
37. *Virginia Bill of Rights*, in Dumbauld, *Declaration of Independence*, p. 168; and rough draft of *Declaration of Independence*, in Becker, *Declaration of Independence*, p. 142.
38. Ellis, *American Sphinx*, p. 57.
39. *Nicomachean Ethics*, published as *The Ethics of Aristotle*. Translated by J. A. K. Thomson, revised by Hugh Tredennick. New York: Penguin Books, 1976, pp. 189–90.
40. Quoted in Dumbauld, *Declaration of Independence*, p. 43.
41. *The Second Treatise of Government*, Thomas P. Peardon, ed. Indianapolis: Bobbs-Merrill, 1952, pp. 4–5.
42. *Second Treatise of Government*, p. 128.
43. Morison, *Oxford History of the American People*, p. 222.
44. Quoted in Introduction to John Locke, *Second Treatise of Government*, p. xx.
45. *Second Treatise of Government*, p. 61.
46. Quoted in Diane Ravitch, ed., *The American Reader: Words That Moved a Nation*. New York: HarperCollins, 1990, p. 41.
47. See Koch and Peden, *Life and Selected Writings of Thomas Jefferson*, p. 22.
48. Ellis, *American Sphinx*, p. 59.
49. Henry S. Commager, "Jefferson and the Enlightenment," in Weymouth, *Thomas Jefferson*, p. 40.
50. Commager, "The Declaration of Independence," in Weymouth, *Thomas Jefferson*, p. 186.
51. See Koch and Peden, *Life and Selected Writings of Thomas Jefferson*, p. 22.

Chapter 4: Congress Debates, Revises, and Signs the Declaration

52. Letter to Abigail Adams, July 3, 1776, in Commager and Morris, *Spirit of 'Seventy-Six*, vol. 1, pp. 320–21.

53. See Koch and Peden, *Life and Selected Writings of Thomas Jefferson*, pp. 22–23.
54. See Koch and Peden, *Life and Selected Writings of Thomas Jefferson*, pp. 22–23.
55. See Koch and Peden, *Life and Selected Writings of Thomas Jefferson*, pp. 24–25.
56. See Koch and Peden, *Life and Selected Writings of Thomas Jefferson*, p. 26.
57. See Koch and Peden, *Life and Selected Writings of Thomas Jefferson*, pp. 26–27.
58. Quoted in Koch and Peden, *Life and Selected Writings of Thomas Jefferson*, p. 21.
59. Quoted in Dumbauld, *Declaration of Independence*, p. 163.
60. Ellis, *American Sphinx*, p. 52.
61. Quoted in Commager and Morris, *Spirit of 'Seventy-Six*, vol. 1, pp. 316–17; Koch and Peden, *Life and Selected Writings of Thomas Jefferson*, pp. 25–26; and Becker, *Declaration of Independence*, pp. 212–13.
62. Letter to Timothy Pickering, August 16, 1822, in Commager and Morris, *Spirit of 'Seventy-Six*, vol. 1, p. 314.
63. Quoted in Koch and Peden, *Life and Selected Writings of Thomas Jefferson*, p. 21. Undaunted by Congress's deletion of the clause, Jefferson remained committed to ending the slave trade. In the fall of 1776, he introduced a bill in the Virginia legislature calling for a ban on the importation of slaves to that state. The bill passed into law two years later. Although this did not stop Virginians from owning slaves, it was an important step in the long process of eliminating the slavery institution altogether.
64. Letter to James Madison, August 30, 1823, in Commager and Morris, *Spirit of 'Seventy-Six*, vol. 1, p. 315.
65. Quoted in Koch and Peden, *Life and Selected Writings of Thomas Jefferson*, p. 21.
66. Letter to James Madison, August 30, 1823, in Commager and Morris, *Spirit of 'Seventy-Six*, vol. 1, p. 315.
67. Letter to James Madison, August 30, 1823, in Commager and Morris, *Spirit of 'Seventy-Six*, vol. 1, p. 315.
68. *Biographical Sketches of Famous Men*, in Koch and Peden, *Life and Selected Writings of Thomas Jefferson*, pp. 178–79.
69. Malone, *Jefferson the Virginian*, p. 222.
70. Peterson, *Thomas Jefferson*, p. 92.
71. Quoted in Commager and Morris, *Spirit of 'Seventy-Six*, vol. 1, p. 311.
72. The actual copy Hancock (and Thomson?) signed, which was probably a handwritten, heavily revised rough draft, has been lost. A

corrected version of the document, appearing in a printed journal kept at the time, bears the words, also in print, "Signed by the order and in behalf of the Congress, John Hancock, President."

Chapter 5: The Widespread Influence of the Declaration's Ideals

73. Quoted in Koch and Peden, *Life and Selected Writings of Thomas Jefferson*, p. 72.
74. Quoted in Simon Schama, *Citizens: A Chronicle of the French Revolution*. New York: Knopf, 1989, p. 48.
75. *Letters*, quoted in Becker, *Declaration of Independence*, pp. 230–31.
76. J. L. Talmon, *Romanticism and Revolt: Europe 1815–1848*. New York: Harcourt, Brace and World, 1967, p. 51.
77. Venezuela's revolutionary congress declared the nation's independence from Spain on July 5, 1811, and the revolutionaries finally defeated and drove out the Spanish in 1821. Miranda was unjustly accused of betraying his comrades, who handed him over to the Spanish. He died in a Spanish prison in 1816.
78. James F. Hoge Jr. and Fareed Zakaria, eds., *The American Encounter: The United States and the Making of the Modern World*. New York: BasicBooks, 1997, p. 9.
79. Quoted in Hoge and Zakaria, *The American Encounter*, p. 3.
80. Quoted in Ravitch, *American Reader*, pp. 202–204.
81. "The Declaration of Independence," in Earl Latham, ed., *The Declaration of Independence and the Constitution*. Boston: D. C. Heath, 1956, p. 8.
82. Ellis, *American Sphinx*, p. 54.
83. J. Franklin Jameson, *The American Revolution Considered as a Social Movement*. Princeton, NJ: Princeton University Press, 1926, p. 9.
84. Gordon S. Wood, *The Radicalism of the American Revolution*. New York: Knopf, 1992, p. 4.

For Further Reading

Isaac Asimov, *The Birth of the United States, 1763–1816*. Boston: Houghton Mifflin, 1974. One of the most prolific and gifted of American popular writers here delivers a highly informative survey of the main events and characters of the American Revolution and early decades of the United States.

Herbert M. Atherton and J. Jackson Barlow, eds., *1791–1991, The Bill of Rights and Beyond*. Washington, DC: Commission on the Bicentennial of the United States Constitution, 1990. This very handsomely mounted book, which is available in most schools and libraries, features many stunning photos and drawings that perfectly highlight the readable text summarizing the impact of the original ten amendments to the Constitution.

Margaret Cousins, *Ben Franklin of Old Philadelphia*. New York: Random House, 1980. The main events and characters of the tumultuous years leading up to the Declaration of Independence are captured in this biography of one of the principal U.S. founding fathers. Aimed at junior high school readers.

Stuart A. Kallen, *The Declaration of Independence*. Edina, MN: Abdo and Daughters, 1994; and R. Conrad Stein, *The Declaration of Independence*. Chicago: Childrens Press, 1995. These two recent, nicely illustrated volumes, which present only the most basic facts about the Declaration, are geared to grade school readers.

Bonnie L. Lukes, *The American Revolution*. San Diego: Lucent Books, 1996. A well-written history of the American war of independence, highlighted by numerous quotes from primary and secondary historical and literary sources describing the conflict and the period. Suitable for junior high, high school, and adult nonspecialist readers.

Don Nardo, *The Bill of Rights: Opposing Viewpoints Digests*. San Diego: Greenhaven Press, 1997; and *The Revolutionary War: Opposing Viewpoints Digests*. San Diego: Greenhaven Press, 1998. These volumes provide a collection of extensively documented essays containing a wide range of opinions and debates about the American war for independence, rights, equality, and the important figures involved.

———, *Democracy*. San Diego: Lucent Books, 1994. This book, which can be used as a companion volume to this one on the Declaration of Independence, traces the origins and development of democratic thought and practice, from ancient Athens and the Roman Republic, through the Magna Carta, the development of the English Parliament, the English Bill of Rights, the ideas of Locke, Rousseau, Montesquieu, Mills, and other advocates of human rights, the American Revolution and the establishment of the U.S. Constitution, the French Revolution, and the spread of democracy in the modern world.

———, *The Importance of Thomas Jefferson*. San Diego: Lucent Books, 1993. A concise biography of Jefferson, including his role as principal author of the Declaration of Independence and other contributions to the formation of the infant United States. Useful for reports and research papers.

Walter Olesky, *The Boston Tea Party*. New York: Franklin Watts, 1993. The events and personalities shaping the famous incident that provoked Parliament into punishing Boston and thereby fatally escalated tensions between the colonies and Britain are recounted here in a simple format for basic readers.

Gail B. Stewart, *The Revolutionary War*. San Diego: Lucent Books, 1991. One of the best current writers for young adults does a fine job chronicling the main events of the war between Britain and its American colonies.

Irwin Unger, *These United States: The Questions of Our Past, Volume I*. Boston: Little, Brown, 1978. Aimed at high school and undergraduate college students, this is one of the best available general, nonscholarly histories of the early United States. Very well written, with excellent production values.

Works Consulted

Primary Sources

The following volumes (or sets of volumes) are comprehensive and invaluable mines of primary source materials, each containing from several dozen to more than a hundred complete or partial documents (letters, pamphlets, newspaper articles, journals, town records, and so on).

Aristotle, *Ethics*, published as *The Ethics of Aristotle*. Translated by J. A. K. Thomson, revised by Hugh Tredennick. New York: Penguin Books, 1976.

Bernard Bailyn, ed., *Pamphlets of the American Revolution*. Cambridge, MA: Harvard University Press, 1965.

Max Beloff, ed., *The Debate on the American Revolution, 1761–1783*. London: Adam and Charles Black, 1960.

Isaiah Berlin, ed., *The Age of Enlightenment: The 18th Century Philosophers*. New York: New American Library, 1956.

Henry S. Commager and Richard B. Morris, eds., *The Spirit of 'Seventy-Six: The Story of the American Revolution as Told by Participants*. 2 vols. New York: Bobbs-Merrill, 1958.

John C. Dann, ed., *The Revolution Remembered: Eyewitness Accounts of the War for Independence*. Chicago: University of Chicago Press, 1980.

John Dos Passos, *John Dos Passos Presents the Living Thoughts of Tom Paine*. New York: Fawcett, 1963.

William Dudley, ed., *The American Revolution: Opposing Viewpoints*. Greenhaven Press, 1992.

Carl J. Friedrich and Robert G. McCloskey, eds., *From the Declaration of Independence to the Constitution: The Roots of American Constitutionalism*. Indianapolis: Bobbs-Merrill, 1954.

Adrienne Koch and William Peden, eds., *The Life and Selected Writings of Thomas Jefferson*. New York: Random House, 1944.

A. A. Lipscomb and A. E. Bergh, eds., *The Writings of Thomas Jefferson*. 20 vols. Washington, DC: Thomas Jefferson Memorial Association of the United States, 1903.

John Locke, *The Second Treatise of Government*. Edited by Thomas P. Peardon. Indianapolis: Bobbs-Merrill, 1952.

Samuel E. Morison, ed., *Sources and Documents Illustrating the American Revolution, 1764–1788, and the Formation of the Federal Constitution*. Oxford: Clarendon Press, 1953.

Richard B. Morris, ed., *The American Revolution, 1763–1783: A Bicentennial Collection*. Columbia: University of South Carolina Press, 1970.

Diane Ravitch, ed., *The American Reader: Words That Moved a Nation*. New York: HarperCollins, 1990.

Alden T. Vaughan, ed., *Chronicles of the Revolution*. New York: Grosset and Dunlap, 1965.

Major Modern Sources

David Ammerman, *In Common Cause: American Response to the Coercive Acts of 1774*. Charlottesville: University Press of Virginia, 1974. An excellent scholarly study of the institution of and reactions to the British measures, called the Intolerable Acts by the colonists, that placed severe restrictions on Boston as retaliation for the Boston Tea Party.

Carl Becker, *The Declaration of Independence: A Study in the History of Political Ideas*. New York: Harcourt, Brace and Company, 1922. A well-written and useful book, thought by many historians to be the most insightful modern volume written about the Declaration.

Julian P. Boyd, *The Declaration of Independence: The Evolution of the Text as Shown in Facsimiles of Various Drafts by Its Author*. Princeton, NJ: Princeton University Press, 1945. This thorough scholarly work is one of the two (the other being Becker's book, above) most often used by historians in analyzing the various drafts of the Declaration.

Gilbert Chinard, *Thomas Jefferson: The Apostle of Americanism*. Ann Arbor: University of Michigan Press, 1966. This scholarly work emphasizes Jefferson's contributions to the formation of American and democratic thought and values.

Edward Countryman, *The American Revolution*. New York: Hill and Wang, 1985. Arguably the most authoritative single-volume general history of the American war for independence, this is a large, richly documented, and engrossing study. Highly recommended.

Eric Foner, *Tom Paine and Revolutionary America*. New York: Oxford University Press, 1976. This biography of the fiery revolutionary who penned the widely influential *Common Sense* effectively covers the social and political panorama of the American colonies of his era. Well written, superbly documented, and generally superior of its kind.

Merrill Jensen, *The Founding of a Nation: A History of the American Revolution, 1763–1776*. New York: Oxford University Press, 1968. Jensen, one of the major historians of the revolutionary period, here explores the writings, speeches, actions, and reactions of the colonists in the formative years of the founding of the United States.

Dumas Malone, *Jefferson the Virginian*. Boston: Little, Brown, 1948. This first volume of Malone's epic, prodigiously researched and documented, and masterfully written six-volume study, widely acclaimed as the most authoritative multi-volume biography of Jefferson, contains much valuable information about Jefferson's early political activities and his drafting of the Declaration of Independence.

Edmund S. Morgan and Helen M. Morgan, *The Stamp Act Crisis: Prologue to Revolution*. Chapel Hill: University of North Carolina Press, 1953. A highly detailed and comprehensive scholarly study of the background of the Stamp Act, British motivations for implementing it, America's irate reactions to it, the act's repeal, and how the crisis foreshadowed the coming struggle between the colonies and the mother country.

Merrill D. Peterson, *Thomas Jefferson and the New Nation*. New York: Oxford University Press, 1970. The best and most authoritative existing single-volume biography of Jefferson, Peterson's work contains a great deal of information about the genesis and completion of the Declaration of Independence. Very highly recommended.

Hugh F. Rankin, *The American Revolution*. New York: G. P. Putnam's Sons, 1964. Rankin, formerly of Tulane University, here effectively covers the highlights of the U.S. war for independence through a chain of long, colorful, and often dramatic eyewitness accounts from the period (each preceded by an informative preface by the author).

Clinton Rossiter, *Seedtime of the Republic: The Origin of the American Tradition of Political Liberty*. New York: Harcourt, Brace and World, 1953. The former widely respected Cornell University scholar won a number of literary awards for this study, an original one for its time, which examines the political ideas that shaped the American Revolution and how those ideas became part of the fabric of the documents and institutions of the infant United States. Will be of interest mainly to scholars and teachers.

Harry M. Ward, *The American Revolution: Nationhood Achieved, 1763–1788*. New York: St. Martin's Press, 1995. A fine, up-to-date, quite detailed overview of the American march toward independence, the struggle with Britain, and the early formative years of the new American nation.

Lally Weymouth, ed., *Thomas Jefferson: The Man, His World, His Influence*. London: Weidenfeld and Nicolson, 1973. An excellent collection of essays about Jefferson, each by a world-class historian. Of special interest here are "Jefferson and the Enlightenment," by Henry Steele Commager, "Prolegomena to a Reading of the Declaration," by Garry Wills, and "The Declaration of Independence," also by Commager.

Additional Modern Sources

George A. Billias, ed., *The American Revolution: How Revolutionary Was It?* New York: Holt, Rinehart, and Winston, 1965.

Stewart G. Brown, *Thomas Jefferson*. New York: Washington Square Press, 1963.

Philip Davidson, *Propaganda and the American Revolution, 1763–1783*. New York: W. W. Norton, 1973.

Edward Dumbauld, *The Declaration of Independence and What It Means Today*. Norman: University of Oklahoma Press, 1950.

Joseph J. Ellis, *American Sphinx: The Character of Thomas Jefferson*. New York: Knopf, 1997.

Thomas Flemming, *1776: Year of Illusion*. New York: Norton, 1975.

Thomas Flexner, *George Washington*. Boston: Little, Brown, 1968.

Richard Hofstadter et al., *The United States: The History of a Republic*. Englewood Cliffs, NJ: Prentice-Hall, 1957.

James F. Hoge Jr. and Fareed Zakaria, eds., *The American Encounter: The United States and the Making of the Modern World*. New York: BasicBooks, 1997.

J. Franklin Jameson, *The American Revolution Considered as a Social Movement*. Princeton, NJ: Princeton University Press, 1926.

Merrill Jensen, *The Making of the American Constitution*. New York: D. Van Nostrand, 1964.

Earl Latham, ed., *The Declaration of Independence and the Constitution*. Boston: D. C. Heath, 1956.

Piers Mackesy, *The War for America, 1775–1783*. Cambridge, MA: Harvard University Press, 1964.

Pauline Maier, *From Resistance to Revolution*. New York: Knopf, 1972.

Edward G. McGrath, *Is American Democracy Exportable?* Beverly Hills: Glencoe Press, 1968.

Samuel E. Morison, *The Oxford History of the American People*. New York: Oxford University Press, 1965.

Henry A. Myers, *Are Men Equal? An Inquiry into the Meaning of American Democracy*. Ithaca, NY: Cornell University Press, 1963.

Simon Schama, *Citizens: A Chronicle of the French Revolution*. New York: Knopf, 1989.

J. L. Talmon, *Romanticism and Revolt: Europe 1815–1848*. New York: Harcourt, Brace and World, 1967.

John C. Wahlke, ed., *The Causes of the American Revolution*. Boston: D. C. Heath, 1950.

Francis G. Walett, *Patriots, Loyalists, and Printers: Bicentennial Articles on the American Revolution*. Worcester, MA: American Antiquarian Society, 1976.

Gordon S. Wood, *The Radicalism of the American Revolution*. New York: Knopf, 1992.

Howard Zinn, *A People's History of the United States*. New York: HarperCollins, 1980.

Index

Picture Credits

Cover photo: Peter Newark's American Pictures
The American Revolution: A Picture Sourcebook by John Grafton, Dover Publications, Inc., 9, 10, 16, 41
Archive Photos, 24
Brown Brothers, 57
Corbis-Bettmann, 63
Library of Congress, 14, 21, 23, 25, 26, 27, 29, 30, 32, 37 (both), 55, 76, 77
North Wind Picture Archives, 17, 19, 35, 36, 50
Stock Montage, Inc., 44, 47, 54

About the Author

Historian and award-winning author Don Nardo has written many books for young adults about American history and government, including *The U.S. Presidency, The U.S. Congress, The Mexican-American War, The Bill of Rights, The Great Depression*, and *Franklin D. Roosevelt: U.S. President.* Mr. Nardo has also written several teleplays and screenplays, including work for Warner Brothers and ABC-Television. He lives with his wife, Christine, and dog, Bud, on Cape Cod, Massachusetts.